CW01500622

The
TREE
and the
MOUNTAIN

About the Author

Jonathan Cave experienced a nomadic childhood, living in five countries before settling in New Zealand to study law. By forty, he was a partner in a prestigious Geneva firm, outwardly successful yet inwardly drained, restless and unable to enjoy the life he had worked so hard to create.

Determined to bridge that gap, Jonathan turned inward, asking himself who he truly was, what mattered most and why he was chasing so hard. This *inside-out* approach helped him move beyond his impostor syndrome and rediscover the clarity, alignment and energy he thought he had lost.

Today, Jonathan is an international leadership coach, guiding people from all walks of life on journeys of self-discovery and growth. *The Tree and the Mountain*, his first allegory, is born of this transformation and invites readers to reflect on their own search for meaning, purpose and authenticity. He is married with two children and loves rugby.

The
TREE
and the
MOUNTAIN

—➤ Dare to Become ◂—

JONATHAN CAVE

Illustrated by Olivia Dhordain

BROWN
DOG
BOOKS

First published 2026

Published under licence by Brown Dog Books and
The Self-Publishing Partnership Ltd, 10b Greenway Farm,
Bath Rd, Wick, nr. Bath BS30 5RL, UK

www.selfpublishingpartnership.co.uk

ISBN printed book: 978-1-83952-983-2
ISBN e-book: 978-1-83952-984-9

Cover design by Blacksheep
Internal design by Mac Style

Printed and bound in the UK

This book is printed on FSC® certified paper

MIX
Paper | Supporting
responsible forestry
FSC® C013604

To the incredible self within each of us,
waiting to be discovered.

Contents

Preface

Nine years ago, I was a lawyer, who had been practising for nearly fifteen years. I spent my days protecting my clients' interests to the best of my ability, which usually consisted in dealing with the latest fire needing to be put out in someone's life. In many ways, I was a firefighter in a suit. That's what it felt like. And it was exhausting.

I was living in a constant state of tension and urgency. My mind never seemed to stop. I had difficulty switching off and relaxing, even on holiday.

Afraid my career and world would come crashing down if I didn't deliver and perform, I worked harder and harder.

I did fewer and fewer of the things I loved – simply no time for that. In fact, I realised that I never had time at all, as if it didn't exist for me. It sounds crazy but it's true.

I was constantly focused on the next 'thing', the next challenge – and once it was achieved would immediately ask myself 'What's next?', as if trying to prove something to someone over and over. But prove what? And to whom? I could not say.

My precious energy was being spent faster than I could replenish it. My 'tank' felt empty. Depleted. What energy I did have was being given to work, and I was bringing the leftovers home to the people I loved the most… my wife and family.

THE TREE AND THE MOUNTAIN

The image of my two young children flashes before my eyes. I can hear their excited voices screaming, 'Daddy! Daddy!' as I would walk through the door every evening. Their mum would be standing behind, watching, and wishing I was coming in happy.

That image hurts more than I can describe. The hope and excitement in their bright eyes contrasting with the tiredness and stress in mine. It felt like a dagger to the heart.

How had I come to this? How had I gone from being a curious, energetic, dynamic young man to the tired, frustrated shadow of his former self who was neglecting those he loved the most?

I had done everything society had asked of me. I paid attention at school, getting good grades. I found little jobs during the school holidays to gain experience and earn some money. I went to university to specialise, before starting at the bottom of the ladder with everything to prove.

I worked hard, trying to over-deliver wherever possible and being helpful even when it was outside my job description.

I progressed quickly with the promise my efforts would lead to 'success', leading to happiness and fulfilment. That was the promise. That was my hope.

And I had achieved the career success part of the equation, becoming a partner in a prestigious law firm. Many of my friends had also done well, becoming business owners, senior executives or well-paid employees. We had 'made it', as they say. At least, that's what it looked like. On the outside.

The truth was, I had an uncomfortable inner feeling cocooned in a comfortable external reality. Yet I felt I couldn't possibly complain or share this feeling of deprivation, even with my closest family and friends. I was privileged – one of the lucky ones. So, I kept my emotions bottled up for as long as I could, throwing myself into work, taking expensive holidays and pretending everything was fine.

Except it wasn't. There was something missing, something fundamental. But what and why? I didn't know. And I wanted to find the answers and a better path forward.

The Tree and the Mountain is a direct result of that quest. It takes the form of an allegory, using symbols and metaphors to communicate profound messages and deeper meaning.

It is very personal, yet it is the story of so many high achievers who, without knowing it, have somehow lost sight of their authentic selves on their journey.

It is a story for those who sense there is an important piece of the puzzle missing in their lives.

It is a story for those who may have achieved some level of external 'success' but have not yet learned to truly enjoy that success deep within themselves.

Ultimately, it is a story for those who seek to live life in a high-energy, high-performing, authentic state, instead of carrying sadness and frustration on their backs.

As you join me on this journey, I invite you to immerse yourself in one of the most extraordinary experiences life offers us: that of discovering, understanding and connecting with the most incredible person you will ever meet...

You.

Jonathan Cave

1

The Lawyer

ndrew's alarm blared at 6.15 a.m., tearing him from sleep with its sharp, familiar sting. Lena groaned beside him. 'You *better* get up this time,' she muttered. 'It's like reliving a nightmare on loop.'

He glanced at his phone, his body heavy with fatigue, and instead of hitting *off*, his finger drifted lazily towards *snooze*. Burying himself deeper into the covers to avoid further judgement, he hoped the world would hold off just a little longer.

At 7.15 a.m., he finally dragged himself up. This was the absolute last moment he could stay in bed until and still make it into the office on time. His mind already racing with the day's demands, he stumbled towards the shower.

By 7.45 a.m., he was three espressos down. He walked over to Lena, who was serving the children their breakfast, and pecked her on the cheek.

'See you when you land,' she said.

He waved to the kids. 'Bye, Audrey... bye, Oliver.'

'Mum!' Oliver protested. 'Audrey's stolen my toast!'

Andrew left the house and slid behind the wheel of his Audi A4 Sport. The growl of the engine when he pressed the starter button never failed to satisfy. It spoke of accomplishment and arrival and the promise of so much more to come. He drove towards Geneva's city centre, the sleek car cutting through the cold November air. The weather was lousy; the late autumn mornings often were.

The radio crackled as he pulled into the underground parking beneath the Mont Blanc Bridge, which divided the city's left and right banks. *'Severe rain forecast for the day...'* announced the cheerful presenter as Andrew parked and stepped out into the biting wind.

A brisk three-minute walk led him to the towering glass entrance of a boutique law firm perched neatly on the fourth floor. He entered, nodded to the assistants and paralegals, and made his way to his office.

His daily routine was comforting and predictable: client requests, meetings, negotiations, and crisis management – defending the interests of successful entrepreneurs. He thrived on it.

Sinking into his chair, he took a rare moment to look out of the window as his computer warmed up, the rain streaking the glass. Geneva wasn't exactly beautiful at this time of year – but life *was*. His life. A flourishing legal career, a wonderful wife, two healthy children and a sprawling house nestled in the suburbs. Would he change anything? *No.* The answer came without hesitation as he typed in his password.

His phone rang, pulling him from his thoughts. The senior partner's name flashed on the screen: *Margot Kellermann.* He picked up immediately.

'Can I see you in the boardroom?'

'Of course,' he answered.

THE LAWYER

Straightening his tie and slipping back into his suit jacket, he walked through the open-plan area, his mind wandering through a thousand possibilities. At one of the desks sat Emile, a young paralegal, looking decidedly glum.

'What's wrong, Emile?' said Andrew. 'You look as if you have the world on your shoulders.'

'It's the acquisition contract for Desplat SA and Coriolus Engineering. The draft's needed by Friday, and I can't get my head around the clauses on intellectual property.'

'Let me take a look with you shortly,' Andrew offered. 'I've just been summoned to a meeting but I'll catch you on the way out.'

Emile brightened. His relief was palpable.

As Andrew approached the boardroom, Margot's PA, Magali, looked up from her laptop and smiled at him more brightly than was usual. 'She's ready for you. Go right in.'

2

The Announcement

To Andrew's surprise, Margot wasn't in her usual place at the big walnut table. Tall and as elegant as ever, she was standing by the window that overlooked the lake and the mighty Jet d'Eau fountain, gazing wistfully. Margot Kellermann didn't do *wistful*. Something big was afoot. It was troubling.

'Hello, Andrew.'

She hadn't looked in his direction nor invited him to sit, so he joined her by the window and looked out over what was arguably the finest boardroom view in Geneva. 'Everything OK?'

'Everything's fine,' she said. 'It just doesn't seem like eleven years since I first took in the view from this room.' She was silent for a moment. 'I need to share something with you – and I trust you'll keep it to yourself for now.'

'Of course.'

'Pascal has acquired a bigger boat. Since his retirement, he's been hankering to try some open ocean sailing. He wants me to go with him. When I get back, it's more nights at the theatre for me – and much more time with my grandchildren. I never saw enough of my daughters when they were growing up. I'm retiring, Andrew.'

THE TREE AND THE MOUNTAIN

This was worrisome. Margot had been a stable element of his career at the firm, frequently demanding but straight-dealing and always dependable. Her replacement could upend all of that. 'When is this happening?'

'Depends on how soon you can step up.'

Andrew's spine tingled. Did she really mean what he thought she meant? He had to be careful – he mustn't embarrass himself.

'What's wrong?' she said. 'Don't you feel ready for the senior partner role?'

And there it was. The words whistled through Andrew's mind like a bullet train... *senior partner*... the holy grail. In a flash, memories surged: his first day at law school... the internships... the late nights... the struggle to climb. And today, he'd just been told he would reach the top of the tree. 'Err... yes... Of course. It's just... Well, I'm just gratified by your confidence in me, Margot, that's all. Thank you.'

'No need. You're well capable and it's no more than you deserve – nobody can question your commitment or how hard you've worked. I'd like you to be up to speed within four weeks – can you do that? I'll give you all the help you need in the meantime. I take it that you *are* up for this?'

'Yes... absolutely!' His head was buzzing. He took a deep breath. He must try to remain level-headed and professional.

'Good. Then off you go and enjoy some space. I'm sure you've a lot to think about. Come back at close of business and we'll run over some formalities.'

When he left the boardroom, Magali's beaming smile was broader than ever. No doubt about it: she *knew* – or at least suspected. *This was real.* He didn't need to pinch himself. In a supreme effort to conceal his excitement, he straightened his face and kept his eyes averted as he returned to his office.

His euphoria was dented by the sight of Emile, who looked at him like a puppy anxious to be taken for a walk after being cooped up at home all day. But this was not a time for the niceties of intellectual property law.

'Sorry, Emile, but something's just come up. I'm going to be tied up for quite a while.'

Emile's shoulders slumped and he looked away.

'You can do this, Emile, I know you can. Take a look at some model clauses and see what might fit with a bit of tweaking. I've got every confidence in you. Worst case, if you still aren't sure by Thursday, we'll try and spend some time on it then, OK?'

'Err… OK,' said Emile, with little conviction.

Back at his desk, Andrew tried to focus on his emails. When he first started reporting directly to Margot, he'd taken some advice from his trusted mentor, Vijay. It was Vijay who had taken Andrew under his wing when he joined the firm.

'What's she like to work for?' Andrew had asked. 'I've heard she's a stickler.'

'She's demanding,' Vijay had said, 'but perfectly decent and fair. She hates missed deadlines, that's for sure. Here's a tip for you… make sure you do today's work today, not tomorrow. Stick to that and you should get along with her just fine.'

From that day on, Andrew had followed Vijay's advice assiduously. It had cost him some late nights but had finally paid off – big time. But now his thoughts kept drifting to the future, and especially to Lena and the kids and his parents, picturing the joy and pride on their faces when he told them.

Then a rare impulsive thought popped into his mind. Lena was working from home that day. He'd go home and surprise her. He informed his assistant, promising to return in a couple of hours, and strode off through the rain-soaked streets. The weather had worsened, the rain belting against the windshield as he exited the underground parking. He drove fast, his foot heavy on the accelerator, mirroring how he lived his life.

As he sped around the final bend towards his home, the Audi's tyres skidded on the slick, wet road. His hands gripped the steering wheel tighter, his heart pounding. Slamming on the brakes, he struggled to regain control, but the car had its own plan, sliding uncontrollably, defying his every move.

Time slowed down. A concrete wall loomed to his right, inching closer with horrifying slowness. He could see every little crack, every imperfection on its surface as he lurched towards it.

The impact was sudden. Violent.

And then... darkness.

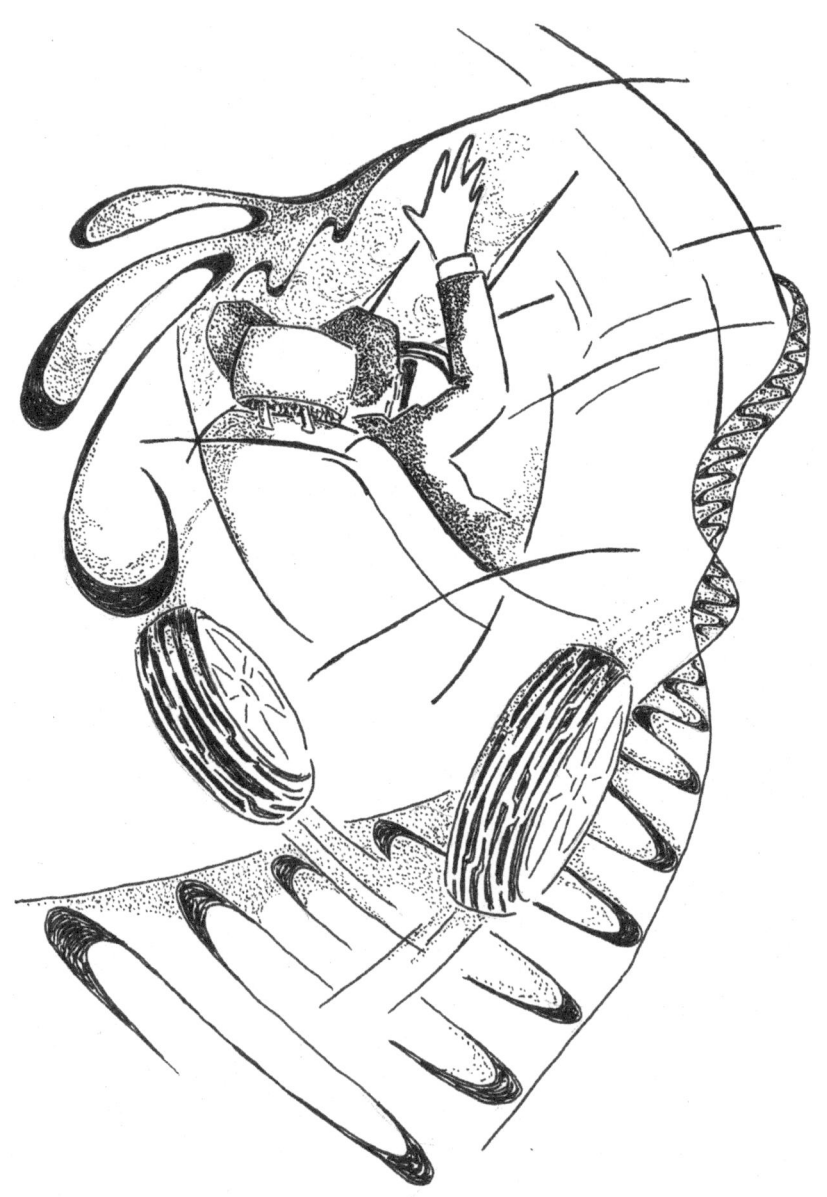

3

The Tree

A ndrew stirred to consciousness, a warm breeze brushing against his face, the faint scent of damp pine filling his nostrils. The rustling of leaves and distant birdsong reached his ears, drawing him further into awareness. A single, pressing question formed in his mind: *Where am I?*

He opened his eyes slowly, blinking against the sunlight. Rough bark pressed against his forehead and nose, and his arms were wrapped around the trunk of a tree. His legs trembled, his feet balanced precariously on two sturdy branches. He was standing up!

He dared to look down – and immediately regretted it. The ground was a dizzying distance below. His heart started pounding like a drum, its rapid beats deafening in his ears. He was so high up. How did he get there? Panic gripped him. His throat tightened and a desperate scream tore from his shaking body: 'Help!'

No response came, the silence only amplifying his terror.

Memories flooded back in fragmented bursts… the screeching tyres… the impact of his Audi colliding with the concrete block. And then… nothing. Where was the wreckage? The ambulance sirens? The cold Geneva rain soaking his skin? The warmth and golden sunlight bathing the tree was unnervingly serene.

He tightened his grip on the trunk, his mind racing to reconcile the impossibility of it all.

As the initial surge of panic ebbed, another thought struck him like a thunderbolt: was he dead? The question lingered, heavy and unshakeable. He had heard stories about near-death experiences – visions of serene landscapes, peaceful limbos that bridged life and death. Was this such a place? Purgatory? A dream? The possibility clawed at him, unsettling and desperately sad.

Tears welled up unexpectedly, blurring his vision. 'Boys don't cry,' he muttered under his breath, thinking of his father – who never cried. He wiped his face with his sleeve, forcing himself to steady his breathing. *Be strong.* But his hands trembled as they clutched the bark, a wave of vulnerability washing over him.

He turned his head slightly and gasped, clinging to one branch. Before him an endless forest stretched to the horizon. A sea of treetops undulated like green waves under the sunlight. It was achingly beautiful, yet utterly overwhelming. The sheer scale of it all made him feel impossibly small, as if he had been swallowed whole by the vastness of the world.

The air hummed with an energy he couldn't place, an unfamiliar aliveness that tingled against his skin. This place was too real to be a dream. Yet the nagging thought persisted: if this wasn't death then what was it? Where *was* he?

The enormity of the situation weighed heavily on him as his mind teetered between grief, fear and a quiet determination to understand. One thing was certain... he needed answers.

THE TREE

4

The Mountain

What now?

Andrew's body remained rigid, his fingers gripping the bark, his breath shallow. Panic threatened to rise again, but he fought to steady himself. He couldn't stay in the tree, that much was certain. But where could he go? What was he supposed to do?

He forced himself to look down again. The dense web of branches stretched beneath him, thick and tangled. His mind flicked through memories like a film reel. Years of relentless studying, the gruelling internships, the climb from junior lawyer to associate and, finally, partner. Every step, another branch. Every test, another rite of passage.

He had climbed. Had always been climbing. Success had been his only direction, his purpose. But now? He was stuck, stranded, perched high up in a tree.

He closed his eyes as a wave of exhaustion swept over him. When he opened them again, he looked up instinctively. One last branch stretched above him, thin and fragile, reaching towards the sky like an arrow. It reminded him of the future he had once envisioned: the title after his name on the door of the plush office next to the boardroom – *Senior Partner*... his private view over the lake and the Jet d'Eau... Was all that still waiting for him or was it lost forever?

THE TREE AND THE MOUNTAIN

He turned slowly, scanning his surroundings. Trees. More trees. An endless world of them, stretching as far as he could see. But then… something caught his eye. Beyond the treeline, beyond the tangled maze, far in the distance, something loomed on the horizon. Immense. Commanding. Its outline sharpened as he focused, almost as if it were drawing closer.

A mountain.

It rose from the land like a silent guardian, pulsing with an inexplicable energy. His breathing slowed. Something about the mountain calmed him. It made no sense, but he felt it deep in his bones; the mountain was calling to him.

And with it came a sudden, undeniable urge: *Leave the tree. Go to the mountain.* He tried to move, but his body refused to cooperate. Why couldn't he move? Why did he feel trapped?

A voice stirred inside him. *Go higher.*

He glanced up at the top branch. Flimsy. Uncertain. But wasn't that his path? Wasn't that what he had always done… climbed higher?

Then, another voice, quieter but firm: *Leave the tree. Look to the mountain.*

More voices followed, rising in a chaotic chorus.

Who do you think you are?

You're in a pickle now, aren't you?

Be responsible. Stay where you are.

They swarmed his mind: parents, teachers, friends – everyone who had ever told him who he was and what he should be. Their words clashed, pulling him in different directions, drowning him in indecision.

THE MOUNTAIN

His breathing quickened. His chest tightened. The clamour was unbearable.

Breathe. A single voice. Soft. Steady. *His own.*

Just breathe.

Closing his eyes, he obeyed, inhaling deeply. The air filled his lungs, expanding his ribcage. He exhaled slowly, feeling the tension loosen its grip. Again… and again… With every breath, the voices faded, the storm inside him quieting into stillness.

When he opened his eyes again, everything looked different.

He looked up at the top branch – and paused.

He looked down at the ground far below – and paused again.

Then, finally, he turned towards the mountain.

His heart pounded – not with fear, but with something else.

Anticipation.

Everything else – the tree, the noise, the fear – fell away. Only he and the mountain remained, a force, pulling him forwards, clear and undeniable. He had his answer.

He began his descent. Branch by branch, he climbed down, his energy returning with every step. The air grew thicker, the earth closer until at last his feet landed softly on the forest floor.

He stood still for a moment, feeling the solidity beneath him, grounded in a way he hadn't felt in years. Then, he turned towards the east. Towards the mountain.

His legs carried him forwards, his steps light yet firm. The pull was irresistible. The deeper into the forest he went, the more the world around him blurred. Trees became shadows and time stretched and folded, minutes or hours lost to the rhythm of movement.

And then… the trees thinned.

The forest parted like a curtain and he stepped into a clearing. There it was. Towering. Magnificent. Its jagged peaks slicing into the clouds. The mountain wasn't just a destination; it was a presence, ancient and unyielding.

'Wow,' Andrew whispered.

It dared him to climb. To uncover its secrets. To find the truth of where he was and why.

Placing one foot on the rocky ground, he looked up at the slopes as they rose above him, twisting out of sight, and took his first step into the unknown.

THE MOUNTAIN

5

First Steps

Andrew's first steps brimmed with hope and curiosity. He zigzagged between the towering trees, stepping over protruding roots and dodging thorny shrubs that clawed at his legs, their tiny hooks snagging his clothes.

The mountain was alive with a quiet energy. Tall spruce and pine trees shimmered in the distance. The ash trees arched overhead, their elegant branches filtering flecks of golden sunlight on the springy moss that blanketed the ground. The scent of damp earth mingled with the crisp, resinous aroma of pine that was borne on the breeze, a fragrance both invigorating and settling.

Somewhere nearby, the soft trickle of water hinted at a hidden stream weaving through the undergrowth. A woodpecker tapped rhythmically against a distant trunk while the rustling of leaves betrayed the presence of small creatures scurrying through the underbrush.

Andrew took it all in as he walked... the scent, the sounds, the coolness of the air touched by the breath of the mountain. Though undefined, the path seemed to unfold before him, inviting him deeper into the unknown.

With every step, the world he knew faded further into the distance. There were no buzzing phones, no relentless deadlines, no constant demands clawing at his attention. Just the whisper of the wind through the branches and the silent, towering presence of the mountain ahead, a sentinel, waiting to reveal its secrets.

Then, without warning, a pang of grief gripped him, sharp and suffocating. His family – his wife, his children – where were they now? A lump rose in his throat. Would he ever see them again? Would he hold Lena close, feel the familiar press of her body against his? Would he hear Oliver's laughter as they competed, pushing each other to the edge of their limits? Would he walk Audrey down the aisle, see the way her eyes shone as she stepped into her future?

His breaths came fast and uneven. He had never truly considered death before. Not like this. He had always been strong, untouchable, built for the fight. He was someone who endured, who conquered. Someone who didn't fall.

And yet here he was. Lost. Alone. Trapped in a place that made no sense, questioning whether he still existed.

A cold fear seeped into his bones. *What if I'm already gone?* The thought struck like a hammer, sending a tremor through his body. If this was death, what kind of place was it? An afterlife? A limbo? Or something worse… nothingness disguised as a dream?

His mind waged war against itself. *No!* He clenched his fists, his nails biting into his palms. He wouldn't accept that – couldn't accept that. He hauled in a deep breath, filling his lungs with the crisp mountain air. This was real. It had to be.

He glanced upwards, desperately seeking something tangible, something solid that could anchor him, prove to him that he wasn't lost in oblivion. His pulse pounded, his eyes scanning.

And then… he saw it up ahead.

A mighty oak tree, ancient and unwavering, its sprawling limbs stretching outwards like the ribs of a vast cathedral. Its thick, gnarled roots twisted deep into the earth, as though they had been there since time began. Unlike the other trees, which swayed gently in the wind, this one stood utterly still and silent, watchful. It exuded a presence, a quiet power that made the forest seem to retreat around it as if in reverence.

Something clicked into place in Andrew's mind, like a puzzle piece he hadn't even realised was missing. This wasn't just any tree. It *meant* something, something familiar…

It called to him – not with words but with a pull so deep and instinctive it bypassed thought entirely. An invitation. A challenge. A moment of clarity.

Andrew inhaled sharply, the fear that had coiled around his chest beginning to unravel. His hands unclenched, and for the first time since waking up in this strange place, he knew exactly what to do.

6

The Oak

As he approached, the oak towered before him, impossibly vast. Its ancient trunk was etched with deep furrows, as though the story of the world was carved into its bark. Though he knew he'd certainly never seen an oak tree so huge, there was something achingly familiar about it. Its countless branches stretched outwards like great arms embracing the sky, whispering with the wind. For how many centuries had this tree stood? How many storms had it weathered?

'It's beautiful, isn't it?'

The voice cut through the quiet like a crack of thunder in a clear sky.

Andrew jolted, his breath catching in his throat. His pulse surged and his body tensed. He spun around, scanning the clearing with wild eyes. The forest was empty. *No one was there.*

For a split second, a terrifying thought gripped him… had the tree itself spoken?

And then… movement.

At the base of the oak, half-hidden by the thick, twisting roots, sat a man. He was leaning against the massive trunk with an ease that suggested he had always been there, waiting. His black hair, streaked with silver, framed a face lined with time, one that seemed to have known both rapturous joy and profound sorrow. His piercing blue eyes shone with an unsettling calm. A simple tunic was draped over his broad shoulders and a beaded bracelet circled his wrist. One hand, calloused and weathered, rested lightly on the exposed roots, as if drawing strength from the ancient giant itself, while the other held a long, stout staff that appeared to be made of ash.

Andrew's breath hitched, his pulse drumming in his ears. *Who was this man?* And – more disturbingly – *how had he not seen him?*

His eyes locked onto those of the stranger, but the man returned his gaze with unsettling ease, his expression unreadable – calm, yet knowing, as though he had been expecting Andrew all along.

For a long moment, neither of them spoke. The forest, the towering oak, the whispering wind… everything seemed to hold its breath.

Then, finally, the old man broke the silence.

'Hello.' His voice was steady, unhurried, cutting through the quiet like the first note of a melody.

Andrew swallowed, his throat suddenly dry. He struggled to respond, his mind scrambling to make sense of what he was seeing. 'H-Hello.' The word sounded awkward, his own voice unfamiliar.

The old man observed him in silence once more.

'Who are you?' The question, which left Andrew's lips before he had time to soften it, was edged with confusion,

THE OAK

wariness – and something else… something raw, just beneath the surface.

The man tilted his head slightly, amusement flickering at the corners of his mouth. His blue eyes gleamed with something Andrew couldn't define – wisdom, perhaps, or the promise of secrets yet to be told.

'I'm an old man sitting under an oak tree,' he said simply, as though that explained everything.

Andrew blinked. 'What are you doing here?'

The man exhaled, resting his hands on the sprawling roots of the oak. 'Waiting.'

'For what?'

'For you, my boy. For you!'

Andrew's breathing faltered. His heart drummed against his ribs, a wild, urgent rhythm. The simplicity of the response only deepened the strangeness of it all.

Fear coiled inside him, cold and relentless, mingling with a terrible, gnawing curiosity. His voice dropped to a whisper, barely more than a breath.

'Am I… dead?'

The old man's gaze sharpened, cutting through him like a blade.

'You are alive,' he said. 'But only just.'

7

New Beginnings

You are alive. But only just.

The words landed like a punch, sending a chill through Andrew's bones. He swallowed hard, his pulse thundering in his ears.

His mind scrambled for logic, something – anything – concrete to hold on to. 'How do you know this?' he asked, feeling decidedly uneasy.

'An excellent question,' said the old man, 'to which, unfortunately, I cannot give you an answer.'

Andrew's brow furrowed. His patience, already frayed, snapped. 'Why not?' Frustration surged through the fear tightening his chest.

The old man's cool gaze was unreadable. 'Because you're not ready to hear the answer.'

Andrew clenched his fists. The vagueness, the calm certainty – it was infuriating. 'How do I even know this is real?' His voice wavered despite himself. 'How do I know you're not just… some hallucination?'

The old man studied him for a moment, then, without a word, extended his hand – palm open, weathered lines catching the dappled light filtering through the oak's branches.

'Pleased to meet you.' His voice was smooth, unwavering. 'I'm Santi.'

Andrew hesitated, the question still clawing at his mind: *Is this real?* But the moment stretched, demanding a different question, one he hadn't dared to ask: *Do I want this to be real?*

Slowly, cautiously, he stepped forwards and clasped the man's hand. It was firm, warm, solid. *Real.* Relief flooded through him, though it did little to settle his storm of thoughts.

'I'm Andrew,' he said warily. 'Pleased to meet you too.' As he stepped back, the sensation of the handshake lingered, grounding him. But questions still roared in his head, unrelenting. He exhaled sharply. 'None of this makes sense.'

Santi chuckled, a rich, knowing laugh. 'Ah, but tell me, Andrew… what in the world truly does?'

Andrew met his gaze, searching for an answer in those deep blue eyes. He found none – only something vast, like the surface of a still lake concealing unknown depths. His voice dropped but remained insistent. 'Where am I?'

Santi gestured to the earth beneath the oak, his movements slow and deliberate. 'Sit,' he said. 'And let's talk.'

Andrew hesitated, but something in the old man's presence compelled him forwards. Slowly, he lowered himself to the ground in front of him. The air between them hummed with something unspoken, something just beyond reach.

Santi studied him quietly for a while, his gaze measured, as though peering *into* him, not at him. Finally, he spoke.

'You are at the beginning, my boy. And it is in new beginnings that everything changes.'

The words settled between them, weighty and deliberate. Andrew gulped. *The beginning of what?* he wanted to ask, but something in the old man's gaze held him still, as if the answer was already unfolding, waiting for him to see it.

Then, without warning, Santi leaned in slightly, his piercing blue eyes locking onto Andrew's. 'Where do you think you are?'

His pulse quickened. The words circled inside him, colliding with the fragments of everything he thought he knew. 'If I'm alive, like you said, then maybe…' The words faltered on his tongue. 'Maybe this is a dream. Or some kind of subconscious state. Maybe I've imagined this oak, this mountain – even you.' His voice barely carried in the stillness. His breathing was shallow and uneven. 'But if I'm not alive…' His throat tightened. '…then maybe I've crossed over. Maybe this is… some kind of bridge to the afterlife.' He forced himself to meet Santi's gaze.

Santi didn't flinch. His expression remained indecipherable, his voice composed. 'You *are* alive, Andrew,' he said, as if chiselling the truth into the air itself. 'And yes, you are within your subconscious, a world just as real – perhaps more real – than the one you are used to. The tree, the oak, the mountain, even me… we are all part of something inside you.'

Andrew frowned. *Inside me?* He thought back to that first moment high up in the tree, the magnetic pull towards the mountain, as if something within him had been guiding his steps.

Santi's voice broke through his thoughts. 'From your tree, you were called to the mountain,' he said. 'And you answered. Why?'

Andrew exhaled, the memory sharp and unshakeable. 'I had to find answers,' he admitted. 'And maybe… a way home.'

Santi studied him for a long moment, his blue eyes holding something deeper than Andrew could grasp. And then, quietly, he asked, 'Is that what you truly want?'

The words struck him like a gong. A flood of images – Lena's smile… the sound of his children's laughter… the warmth of his son's high-five after a win – rushed through him, gripping his chest with a fierce ache.

'More than anything,' he whispered. 'Can you help me?'

Santi smiled.

'I can.'

8

The Quest

Relief flooded through Andrew, his lungs refilling as if he had been holding his breath for hours. But before the sensation could settle, Santi's tone shifted, growing heavier.

'To see your family again, you must climb this mountain.'

Andrew straightened. *Climbing?* That was familiar territory. It was what he did. His life had been one relentless ascent – higher, faster, stronger. Success was always just one more peak away. He looked up at the mountain. *How hard could it be?*

Santi caught the flicker of confidence in Andrew's face and smiled knowingly. 'But it's no ordinary climb, Andrew.'

'What do you mean?'

'For every step you take up the mountain, you will be invited to descend deeper within yourself,' Santi explained. 'The higher you climb, the more you will uncover within. The more you uncover within, the higher you will climb.'

Andrew's mind worked furiously to piece it together. 'So... it's not just physical,' he murmured. 'It's a journey inside myself?'

Santi smiled. 'Exactly so.'

Andrew hesitated, something tightening in his gut. 'And what will I find there?'

Santi held his gaze, his expression unwavering. 'Everything you've ever climbed for,' he said softly. 'And everything you've been running away from.'

Andrew swallowed dryly. He had never run from anything in his life. He was the guy who faced challenges head-on, who pushed through, who conquered. But Santi's words implied that there were truths buried deep within him, uncomfortable truths that he had subconsciously avoided.

'But there's more.' Santi's voice darkened, and a shadow seemed to pass over his face. 'Whether you conquer the mountain or not will determine whether you live or die.'

The air thickened, the significance of his words suffocating. Andrew's breathing quickened and his hands trembled at his sides. 'Die?' he whispered. 'Die on this mountain? Or die for real?'

Santi's expression didn't change. 'Both.'

The world tilted. This wasn't just about finding his way home. This was about everything. His family. His career. His very existence.

THE QUEST

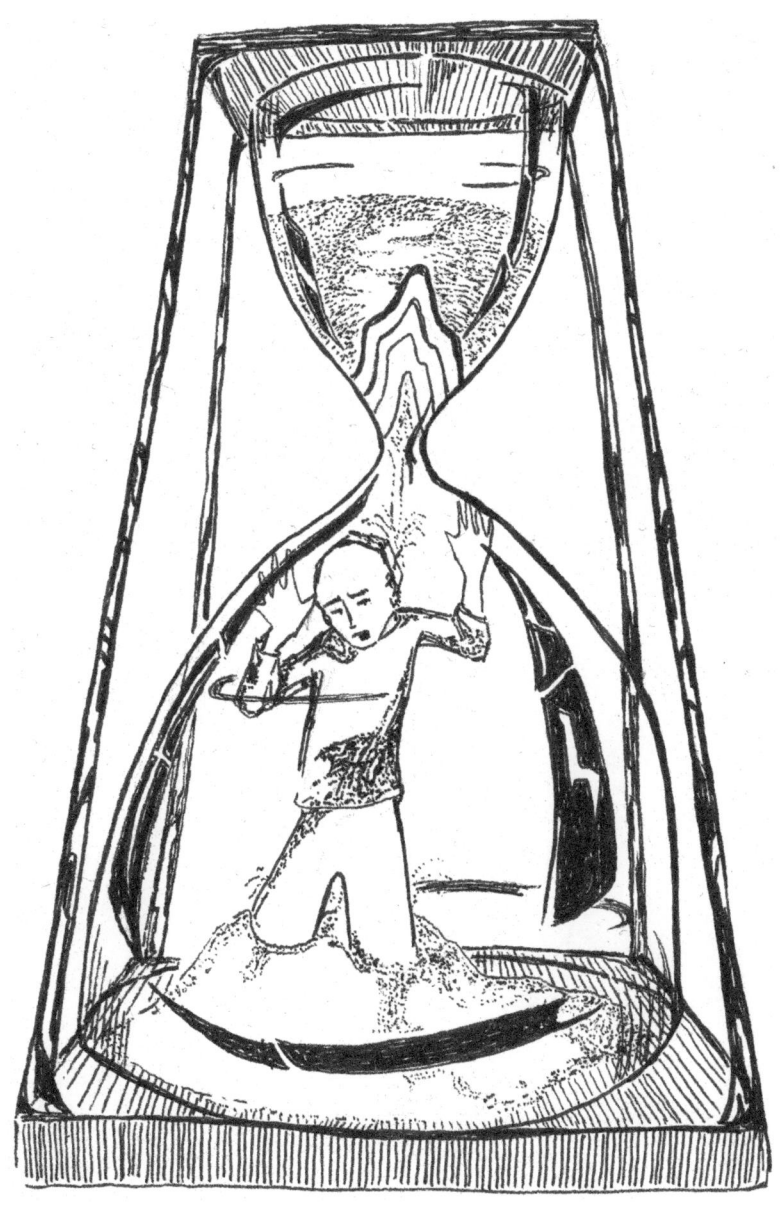

9

Dreams

'How long do I have?' Andrew asked.

'Two days and a night,' the old man said. 'Maybe a little more. Maybe a little less.'

'And how long will it take to climb the mountain?'

'Two days and a night. Maybe a little more, maybe a little less.'

'Then there's no time to lose, is there?' Andrew said, pushing himself up from the ground. 'It's been good talking with you and you've been very kind and helpful. But now I need to press on.'

Santi leaned forwards and placed his hand on Andrew's shoulder. 'But it's not as simple as putting one foot in front of the other,' he said. 'This is the realm of your subconscious – remember?'

Andrew felt a growing sense of impatience. At the risk of offending the old man, he desperately needed to press on. His life and the future of his family depended on it.

'Your journey is mental as well as physical,' said Santi. 'It's not just the visible landscape that you must explore. Your life was slowly but surely drifting away from you. You were—'

'My life was snatched away by a wet road and a concrete wall!' Andrew snapped. 'And everything you've told me only goes to show how urgent it is that I get back to it. *And* it was a good life. A rich and full life – by most people's standards, anyway. And it was just about to get even better!'

'If your life was that wonderful,' said Santi, 'why were you not more eager to embrace it each morning?'

Where was this leading? He had just about had enough. The old man was becoming an impediment and an irritant.

'Tell me about the *snooze* button,' Santi said. 'The one you press on your phone two or three times before getting out of bed. Is your professional life really so exhausting that those extra minutes make such a difference? If they do, surely you could set the alarm for later and jump up, raring to go.'

Andrew's eyes narrowed as he regarded the old man in front of him. 'Look, I really don't see what that has to—'

'Humour me, Andrew. Just this once. Then you can set off if you want to – with me or on your own. Why do you press the snooze button?'

'All right, if you insist,' said Andrew with a sigh. 'It's just an innocent indulgence of mine. Often, in the mornings, my half-conscious mind drifts and takes me places – places that are so warm and comforting or so fascinating or so beautiful that I hate being dragged away. I press the *snooze* button in the hope that I can stay longer. It never works. I always end up somewhere else and the cycle begins again.'

'And where were you taken this morning?'

'Oh, I don't know. I…' Ordinarily, the merest echoes of Andrew's early-morning reveries would evaporate before he had even reached the kitchen. But he was surprised to find that he had a clear recollection of where they had taken him that morning.

'First, I was walking through a steep-sided valley. It had a stark beauty, and I was fascinated by what I might see around every bend. Eventually, I came to the most spectacular waterfall I'd ever seen, cascading into a crystal-clear lake. I had to swim in it, so I stripped off my clothes. I was just about to jump in when the alarm went off. I wanted to find my way back to that lake, so I pressed *snooze*.'

'And did you? Get back to the lake?'

'It never happens that way. I just lay there for a while and drifted off, this time finding myself in the garden of my boyhood home. There was an oak tree – in many ways like this one, only smaller. My father was there, smiling as he put the finishing touches to a tree house. It looked so beautiful to me, almost magical – painted yellow with red windows. He hadn't fitted a ladder yet, so he lifted me up in his strong arms. I was desperate to see inside but before I could climb in, the alarm sounded. I pressed the *snooze* button again. I knew that I wouldn't return to the garden, of course, but I wanted to think about the tree house a while longer and picture my father when he was still young and I was still small.'

'Did the tree house ever exist?'

'No.' Andrew felt a lump in his throat, like a dry crust that couldn't be swallowed. He recalled a time when he was seven years old and his brother Edward was around five. His father had taken turns with them, lifting them onto one of the oak tree's stout horizontal boughs and holding them there before swinging them back down again. He had been spending some time with them before a taxi arrived to whisk him off to the airport for yet another business trip.

'You know what this tree needs, boys? A tree house! Wouldn't that be great? As soon as I get back from Kuala Lumpur, that's what we'll do… build a tree house!'

His father returned home within what seemed like a couple of weeks, but the tree house never materialised. Instead, he remembered a time when his parents seemed distant and cold with one another. Not long after, his father left home for good. In the years that followed, Andrew never forgot that last day in the garden with his father and brother. And he made himself a promise: if he ever had a house, a garden and children of his own, he'd build them a tree house.

Santi's voice broke through Andrew's reverie. 'So, what came next? Did you manage to stay awake?'

'Not then. I soon drifted off. This time I was in some vast Gothic building – like a castle or cathedral, only bigger. There were so many courtyards and towers and rooftops and halls and corridors. The odd thing is that some of the interiors were a fantastical hotchpotch of familiar places – my old school, my university or even the firm's offices in Geneva. Some were deserted, while others teemed with people, most of whom I knew from various stages of my life. Sometimes it seemed that I was alone. At other times, Lena was with me. I was looking for someone – my brother, Edward. I needed to tell him something – I can't remember what. I kept glimpsing him up ahead and I tried to catch up. Something or somebody always got in my way… an obstruction or the

DREAMS

press of crowds, or somebody would waylay me, needing my attention. Eventually, I got within a few yards of him and called out. Just as he was turning around, the alarm went off. No more time to snooze. I knew I had to get up for work.'

'Tell me about your brother,' Santi said. 'Where is he now?'

'Sardinia. When he left university, he got a traineeship with a prestigious bank in Zurich. We used to visit each other often and his career seemed to be thriving. His passion, though, was scuba diving. He'd take diving vacations around the Med whenever he could. Three years ago, he took a trip to Sardinia and never came back. He'd met and fallen in love with a local girl and they eventually started a diving school. It was a struggle at first, but now they earn enough to get by and raise their twin girls. He's always been a laid-back, contented guy and he seems to have everything he wants. In some ways I envy him.'

'I suppose that's some sort of an admission,' Santi said. 'When did you last see Edward?'

'Three years ago.' Andrew felt a warm flush spread across his face. 'He's invited us there on many occasions. Until now, there's never been an ideal time to take him up on his offer.'

Santi raised an eyebrow.

'Ah! But we're going this September,' Andrew announced defensively. 'It's all planned.' And then he remembered that he was soon to become the new senior partner. 'Hmm… that said, it just might have to…'

Santi's eyebrow hadn't moved.

Suddenly, a deep sense of shame filled him – and a yearning to see his brother and meet his nieces and Edward's fiancée for the first time. 'We're going,' he said. 'If I ever reach home, we're going as planned, come what may.'

'Why?' asked Santi. 'To gratify me or to purge your guilt?'

'Neither,' said Andrew, firmly. 'We're going partly because Lena and the kids are looking forward to it. Mostly because Edward is my brother and I love him.'

'Good,' Santi said. 'Then I'm gratified anyway.'

'I'm sorry for losing my patience with you,' said Andrew. 'I hope you'll forgive me.'

Santi smiled warmly. 'There's nothing to forgive, my boy. You've had… an *interesting* morning. You actually seem to be coping rather well. Now, I'll help you as much as I can to return to your life and your family. To do that, we have two realms to explore… the one you can see before you and the one you can't. Are you sure you're willing to do that with me?'

Andrew nodded. 'I am.'

10

Identity

'Where do we begin?' Andrew asked, his voice edged with urgency as it cut through the stillness. The wind stirred in response, rustling the leaves above as if nature itself awaited the answer.

Santi's expression softened into a faint, knowing smile. 'When we first met, you asked me who I was, and I answered,' he said. 'Now, perhaps it's time you told me, in your own words… who you are?'

Andrew opened his mouth, ready to give the answers he had always relied on. *Lawyer. Husband. Father.* But as the words formed on his tongue, something inside him resisted; they felt too small, too rehearsed. He had worn them like armour his whole life, yet here, in this place, they felt hollow.

A lump rose in his throat. Lowering his gaze to the earth beneath him, he searched for an anchor. The silence stretched between them, expectant.

'I…' He exhaled, the truth sinking in. 'I don't really know.' The admission felt greater than he expected.

Santi smiled, his blue eyes unwavering. 'Then tell me what you *do* know.'

Andrew hesitated. He had spent a lifetime mastering facts, presenting airtight arguments. But speaking about *himself…* that was different.

He glanced up at the higher reaches of the mountain, still shrouded in mystery. He drew in a slow breath, filling his lungs with the crisp, pine-scented air. And then, feeling as though the forest itself was urging him forwards, he began to speak.

'I was born in Switzerland, a land of high mountains and deep valleys.' His eyes glazed over, memories unfurling. 'My parents were expats – my father worked in marketing and my mother was a teacher. It was a happy childhood at first. But, when I was eight, everything changed. My parents divorced.'

He paused, the words catching in his throat. He hadn't spoken about this in years.

'My brother Edward and I stayed with my mother. We moved a lot after that – different countries, different schools. By the time I was eighteen, I had lived in five countries. Each one became home for a while, but with every move, I left behind friendships, familiarity – pieces of myself. I learned to adapt. To say goodbye.' He swallowed hard. 'But the more I moved, the less I felt I truly belonged anywhere.'

A soft breeze stirred.

'Mum was always there. Strict, but supportive. Dad… he was in another part of the world. I missed him. No holiday visits could ever fill the void.' His voice dropped, almost to a whisper. 'That void is still there.'

Santi remained silent, letting the echoes of Andrew's words settle between them.

'Entering adulthood, I kept moving – travelling, chasing experiences. It was my way of coping, of filling the emptiness. But I was searching for something, even if I didn't know what.' His brow furrowed slightly. 'Eventually, I became a lawyer. Maybe because it gave me the structure I never had from my father. I moved back to Switzerland and built a career helping entrepreneurs grow and protect their businesses.'

He stopped.

The crash flashed vividly through his mind – the screeching tyres... the wall... the feeling of absolute powerlessness.

'Before the accident,' he continued, quieter now, 'I had just been offered senior partnership. I was about to reach the top of my... *career tree.*' The image of the tree he had clung to for dear life appeared in his mind. Was that what he'd been standing on, gripping onto so tightly? His career tree?

He exhaled slowly, his thoughts shifting from his work to his family. 'I have a wife, Lena, and two children – Oliver and Audrey,' he said softly, their faces filling his mind. 'They're my world.'

Santi studied him, his eyes filled with something Andrew couldn't quite grasp – understanding, maybe, or something deeper.

'Thank you for sharing your story,' Santi said after a moment, his voice as gentle as the wind that whispered through the trees. 'You have given me a great gift. And for that I am deeply grateful.'

Andrew blinked. A gift? He had never thought of his story in that way. He lowered his head in acknowledgement.

A comfortable silence settled over them, the kind that carried meaning. Andrew felt lighter, as if speaking of his past had loosened something deep inside him.

THE TREE AND THE MOUNTAIN

'You've travelled far, Andrew,' Santi said at last. 'You have learned to master the world around you – the world of action, achievement and external success. But now it is time to discover another world... the world within you.'

'What will I discover?' said Andrew.

Santi's gaze held his, as firm as the ancient oak. 'The strength to climb this mountain. The clarity to see the unseen. And, most importantly, the ability to discover who you really are.' His fingers brushed against the beaded bracelet on his wrist.

Andrew looked at the bracelet, observing how beautiful it was. Anticipation swirled within him, tangled with doubt, curiosity and the flicker of something else... something close to hope.

11

Nature's Energy

As he glanced up at the towering oak above them, its colossal branches stretching skywards like ancient arms cradling the heavens, vibrations coursed through Andrew's body. The tree felt alive – not just part of the forest, but the beating heart of it.

Santi's fingers lightly brushed the tree's exposed roots, as if drawing strength directly from the earth itself. He said nothing at first, allowing silence to settle between them, full and rich. The rustling of leaves, the rhythmic hum of unseen life… it all felt amplified, as if the world was holding its breath.

Finally, Santi spoke, his voice loaded with quiet revelation. 'Look at this oak, Andrew. What do you see?'

Andrew contemplated the thick, gnarled roots that burrowed deep into the earth. Acorns lay scattered at the base of the tree, nestled in the damp soil. The trunk was a tapestry of time, furrowed with age. His eyes traced the branches upwards as they stretched towards the sky, their leaves a mix of deep green and golden hues, shimmering where the sunlight touched them.

'It's beautiful,' Andrew murmured, almost reverently. 'I see roots, a trunk, branches… and leaves.'

Santi nodded but remained silent, letting Andrew's thoughts take shape. Something about the roots drew Andrew's focus, the way they gripped the earth.

'What do you see in the roots?' Santi asked, his voice a quiet nudge.

Andrew hesitated then leaned in, as if the answer lay just beneath the soil. 'They anchor the tree,' he said slowly, his thoughts crystallising as he spoke. 'They keep it standing, no matter how fierce the storm.'

A small smile played at the edges of Santi's lips. 'Exactly. The roots keep it connected to something greater than itself. And tell me, Andrew… what keeps *you* grounded when life's storms strike?'

The question struck something deep within him. His mind flicked through memories… his parents' divorce… the constant moving… the relentless chase for success. What had secured him? What had been his foundation?

Then, the answer surfaced, clear as day. 'My values,' he said, the word settling into the space between them. 'They stabilise me. They anchor me.'

Santi gave a slow nod of approval. 'Yes. Our values are our roots. They connect us to what truly matters… our families… our purpose… our identity. Without them, we are easily uprooted.'

Andrew sighed, the truth of it sinking in. His values stretched beneath him like unseen roots, holding him steady even when he hadn't realised it.

'What else do you see?' Santi's voice carried the promise of another lesson waiting to unfold.

Andrew tilted his head back, following the branches as they reached outwards and upwards. But it was the leaves that caught his attention – the way they fluttered in the breeze, drinking in the sunlight. 'The leaves,' he said, softly. 'They reach for something... for the light.'

Santi's smile deepened. 'Yes. The leaves capture light through photosynthesis and transform it into an energy that sustains not just the tree itself but nearly all life on Earth. And you, Andrew? What is your light? What fuels you, often without you even realising it? What helps you impact the world around you?'

Andrew frowned. He had spent so much of his life *doing* that he had never truly stopped to consider *the source...* that gave him energy... that kept him moving... that impacted those around him.

Then it came to him, as natural as breathing. 'My talents,' he said, the realisation settling over him. 'The things I do instinctively. The things that come naturally to me.'

Santi's nod was barely perceptible. 'Like the tree, you have gifts within you, natural abilities that fuel you and, whether you realise it or not, serve others. Your talents are your photosynthesis. They are your contribution, without you even being conscious of it.'

Andrew felt a quiet warmth rise in his chest. His talents weren't just skills or things he had worked hard to master; they were part of *him*, as essential as breathing, his invisible energy at work.

Santi looked up towards the branches. 'And the branches? What do you see in them?'

Andrew considered the twisting limbs stretching outwards – expanding, never still. 'They're always growing,' he murmured. 'Reaching out into the world.'

He imagined the oak as a sapling, fragile yet determined, pushing skywards despite the gravity of the Earth pulling down on it. It had never stopped growing, never stopped expanding into the space above and beneath it. 'The tree knows where it's going.' He felt on firmer ground now.

Santi's eyes gleamed with quiet pride. 'And what about you, Andrew? What helps *you* know where you're going?'

Andrew thought of his relentless drive, his pursuit of success, the goals that had shaped his path. He thought of his family, the life he had built, and the dreams that still lingered in his heart. 'My aspirations.' It was as though the word had been waiting for him to find the answer. 'They guide me.'

Santi's smile broadened. 'Exactly. A tree grows towards the sun, its ultimate source of energy. And you… you grow towards your aspirations, your purpose. These things shape the person you are becoming.'

Andrew sat in stunned silence as the pieces fell into place. The oak wasn't just a tree… it was *him*. It was life.

He had roots – his values – that stabilised him.

He had leaves – his talents – that sustained him and created impact

He had branches – his aspirations – that pulled him forwards, towards growth, giving him direction.

The old man watched him knowingly, as if he had been waiting for this moment. 'You're beginning to understand,' he said softly, his voice carrying an ancient gravity. 'The

NATURE'S ENERGY

more we connect with nature, the more we discover our *own* nature.'

Andrew let the words wash over him, feeling the power of a universal truth revealing itself. *The more we connect to nature, the more we discover our own nature.*

For the first time in a long time, he felt *connected* – not just to the forest around him, but to himself.

Nature wasn't just something around him. It was something *within* him.

And it had been all along…

12

Alignment

Andrew inhaled deeply, the scent of pine and earth wrapping around him, anchoring him in the present while pulling him into the past. Memories surfaced of long summer days spent in nature: the salty sting of ocean air on his skin, the icy shock of mountain streams. He remembered how time had once felt endless, how the world had moved with a slower, more deliberate rhythm.

Unfortunately, that peace had never lasted. As soon as he returned to everyday life, the stillness vanished – drowned out by schedules, responsibilities and the relentless pursuit of something 'more'. The ache of that loss swelled in his chest, sharp and insistent.

Andrew turned to the old man. 'What is this energy I feel in nature, Santi?' he asked. 'And how can I tap into it?'

Santi's fingers traced the roots of the oak before touching his bracelet. Then, with quiet purpose, he began.

'Every person carries three energies within them, Andrew.'

Andrew leaned in slightly. 'Three energies?'

Santi pressed his palm against the roots. 'The first is *foundational* energy, the force that grounds you. It keeps you secure when life's storms rage, securing you to something deeper. It is your *values*.'

In a sweeping gesture, he indicated the massive leafy branches above. 'The second is *transformational* energy, the force that fuels your growth, your ability to contribute and create. Your *talents*.'

Santi pointed at the golden light filtering through the canopy. 'And the third is *directional* energy, the force that guides you, pulls you towards something greater. Your *aspirations*.'

'And when all three converge...' Santi's voice dropped to a mere whisper. '...you discover your central alignment line.'

'My what?' Andrew blurted, his thoughts snapping like a taut wire.

Santi traced a slow, deliberate vertical line in the air, from his head to his chest. 'Your central alignment line,' he repeated, each word measured. 'An invisible vertical axis that runs through the core of your being. It is where your energies *align*, where your *true self* lives. Beneath the noise... beneath the masks.'

Andrew's breathing quickened. 'Why have I never heard of this before?'

Santi's smile was knowing, patient. 'Because from a very young age, we are taught to look outside of ourselves, Andrew. We learn information and processes at school, and chase success and validation in the workplace. But the alignment you seek, the *truth* of who you are, has always been *within*.'

A shiver ran through Andrew. A door had cracked open inside him. 'And what happens when you find this central alignment line?' He felt a surge of excitement. 'What happens then?'

ALIGNMENT

Santi leaned forwards, his beaded bracelet catching the light. 'You tell me, Andrew. Imagine you are living true to your *values* on a daily basis. Imagine you are expressing your *talents* fully, without hesitation. And imagine you are constantly moving towards achieving your *aspirations*. What energy state would you be in?'

Andrew didn't hesitate. 'High energy for sure.'

'Would you be performing at your best or your worst?'

'My best.'

'And would you be your *true self* or pretending to be someone else?'

Andrew exhaled slowly, realisation settling over him like sunlight breaking through clouds. 'My true self.'

Santi smiled, satisfaction flickering in his eyes. 'Exactly. When your energies align, you step into your high-performing, high-energy, authentic self. It's not something you *create* – it's something you *uncover*. It's who you've *always been*.'

Andrew's pulse quickened. He could feel it now. The line wasn't just a concept; it was real. As real as the roots beneath the oak, as real as the branches reaching for the sky.

'Are you ready to find your central alignment line?' asked Santi, pushing himself to his feet.

Andrew rose with him, in anticipation – *readiness*.

'Yes,' he said excitedly, eager to discover his natural energy within.

13

Values

Andrew and Santi walked along the narrow mountain path in silence. Towering trees lined the way, their branches seeming to wave at them gently as they passed.

Santi broke the silence, his voice calm and deliberate. 'Let's begin with your foundational energy. Your values. What do they mean to you?'

Andrew looked up at the dappled sunlight filtering through the canopy as he considered the question. 'They're what's important to me,' he said finally. 'My non-negotiables. What guide me every day.'

Then Andrew thought of Emile, the young paralegal. He pictured him struggling with the acquisition contract, stressed and panicked as the deadline loomed. He hoped Emile had found the courage to seek help. He hoped he'd gone to Vijay, who was infinitely patient and encouraging.

'Something's troubling you,' Santi said.

Andrew nodded sheepishly. 'I was wondering about my values. This morning, somebody asked for my help. I didn't give it. It might have taken me less than half an hour.' Another thought struck him. 'Who knows... if I'd taken the time to help him, perhaps I wouldn't have ended up here.'

'Perhaps,' said Santi. 'And perhaps not. You may have come by another means. The mechanisms of fate are complicated. You should remember also that your guilt and discomfort about what happened this morning prove that you *have* values.'

'It's not enough, though, is it?'

'No, but it's an essential beginning. Values are what matter to us. We use them as our moral compass. They shape our decisions, condition our behaviours and drive our actions. They anchor us when life throws chaos our way.' He glanced at Andrew. 'Have you ever identified some of your values before?'

Andrew pulled up sharply, the realisation landing like a heavy stone in his chest. 'No,' he admitted. 'No, I haven't.'

'Then, let's do it now.' Santi halted beneath the shade of an ash tree and leaned his staff against its trunk. 'Are you ready to uncover your three core values?'

'Why three?'

Santi's lips curled into a small, knowing smile. 'Three is a powerful number. It creates balance and clarity. It's simple, yet complete.'

Andrew nodded, willing to accept the logic.

'Close your eyes,' Santi instructed. 'Place your hands over your heart.'

Andrew hesitated. But something in Santi's tone softened his resistance. Closing his eyes, he rested his hands over his chest. After a few moments, he sensed the regular rhythm of his heartbeat.

VALUES

'Take three deep breaths.' Santi's voice was like a gentle current. 'Let your breathing guide your attention inwards. Let go of the noise. Listen to the silence.'

Andrew inhaled deeply, the mountain air filling his lungs, his shoulders relaxing as the tension drained from him.

'Picture your favourite place in the world,' Santi said softly. 'It can be a place from your youth or somewhere you have holidayed – or anywhere, in fact. A place where you have always felt at peace.'

Almost instantly, Andrew visualised his favourite place: the Barmaz Valley in the Swiss Alps.

'Immerse yourself completely in this special place,' Santi whispered, 'as if you were there right now.' His voice was becoming more distant.

The alpine meadows came into view: the cows grazing among the wildflowers, their bells chiming as they moved. Andrew scanned the forested hillsides cradling the valley and the towering peaks watching over the land like silent guardians of the Garden of Eden. He felt the warmth of the sun on his face and the cool breeze brushing his skin. Time seemed to stretch infinitely in this sacred place that meant so much to him. It was so real, as if he had stepped into the valley itself.

'Now, from this special place, look up into a blue sky cradling a radiant sun.' Santi's voice guided him. 'And across this sky, imagine your first name being written in your own handwriting, in white.'

Andrew saw it... his name, *ANDREW*, etched in glowing letters against the endless blue.

THE TREE AND THE MOUNTAIN

VALUES

'Beneath it,' Santi continued, his voice now softer, almost hypnotic, 'imagine three words appearing... your core values... the essence of who you are. Now... this is important... ask your heart to reveal them to you, one by one – and then wait. Do not seek them. If you do, you will go into the mind. Instead, let them come to you. Be patient.'

Andrew inhaled deeply, feeling the cool mountain air expand his chest, then exhaled slowly, sinking into the moment. At first, the surface of his mind rippled with thoughts – restless, churning, words tumbling over each other like waves in a storm. What were his values? What if he got this wrong? His rational mind clawed for control, grasping at possibilities.

But he followed Santi's advice, staying patient. After taking another deep breath, he exhaled even more slowly this time, letting go of the noise.

And then... he began to descend.

The surface thoughts, loud and frantic, started to drift away, like debris floating on the tide. With each breath, he sank deeper, slipping below his daily worries, past the surface tension of what was expected, what was rehearsed.

Twenty-five metres down...

The world above blurred. The sound of the wind faded, replaced by the rhythmic pulse of his breathing. It was quieter here, yet his thoughts still flitted about – whispers of ambition, of duty, of the roles he had played all his life. Lawyer. Husband. Father. They swirled around him, familiar but suddenly... *weightless*. Not false, but not the whole truth either.

THE TREE AND THE MOUNTAIN

Fifty metres down…

The further he sank, the more the external world dissolved, and in its place something more primal, rawer, awaited. The quiet here was alive, humming with something deeper than words. His heartbeat slowed, synchronising with a rhythm that felt ancient, like the deep currents of the ocean or the stillness of an untouched forest.

Here, in this sacred space, the searching stopped. There was nothing to chase, nothing to force. The answers were already there, waiting.

And then – they rose.

Three simple values, soft but undeniable, rising through the depths like beams of light piercing dark water.

LOVE

Warmth spread through him like the golden glow of morning light touching his skin. Love was not just something he gave; it was the force that connected him to life itself. It had always been his foundation.

HONESTY

A sharp clarity followed, cutting through the haze like a blade. Honesty with others but also with himself. The need to be real, to strip away pretence, to stand in his truth without fear.

MAKING A DIFFERENCE

The final value emerged, steady and unwavering. It was his core driver, the invisible current that had always pulled him forwards. To contribute. To leave a mark. To give more than he took.

VALUES

His eyes snapped open, his breath catching as he returned to the surface. The world around him came rushing back: the rustling trees, the golden light filtering through the leaves, the scent of earth and wood. But something had changed.

The words remained, vivid and undeniable, etched into his being.

He had not found them.

They had found him…

14

Bridging the Gap Within

Santi contemplated Andrew with an air of calm. 'How do you feel?'

Andrew let out a long, slow breath. 'Grounded.'

'Did your values come to you?'

'Surprisingly, yes. But only once I had quietened the noise.'

Santi's eyes glinted with approval. 'It takes silence to truly hear.'

Andrew smiled.

'Tell me, Andrew. What came to you?'

Andrew spoke them aloud, each word landing with a newfound resonance. '*Love... Honesty... Making a difference.*'

'Would you like to reflect on them with me?'

Andrew smiled. 'Love because it's the centre of everything. It's what drives me – to connect, to give, to experience life fully.'

'And honesty?'

Andrew frowned slightly, searching for the right words. 'It's about being real. I try to be truthful with others and with myself. I value authenticity. Dishonesty I can't stand.'

'And making a difference?'

Andrew paused, appearing more subdued. 'I've always wanted to help people. To contribute something meaningful. To leave the world better than I found it.'

Santi studied him carefully. 'Now, let me ask you three more questions.'

Andrew straightened. 'Go ahead.'

Santi looked directly into Andrew's eyes. 'Do you allow yourself the same love you give to others?'

Andrew blinked, caught off guard. His mind raced through memories... self-doubt, relentless self-criticism, the endless striving to be better. 'No,' he admitted quietly.

'Are you honest with yourself?'

Andrew's stomach clenched slightly. 'Not always.'

'And finally...' Santi's voice was gentle yet firm. 'Are you making a difference in your relationship with yourself?'

Andrew looked down at the forest floor. 'I try... but it's hard.'

Santi's smile was warm, patient. 'To understand why I asked you these three questions, consider this... a value is one energy.' He raised a single clenched fist.

'When you apply your values outwardly, to others, but neglect to apply them inwardly, to yourself, you divide that energy. You create a split.' He created a second fist, holding them apart. 'And in that split a gap forms, which in turn creates a tension. That tension weakens you over time because it consumes rather than generates energy for you.'

Andrew watched as Santi slowly brought his fists back together.

'But when you live your values fully, meaning outwardly and inwardly, they align. And when they align...' He locked his fingers together, his hands becoming one. '...they become a powerful, unshakeable force on your *central alignment line.*'

Andrew let the words settle.

'Treat yourself with the same love, honesty and care you give to others, Andrew,' Santi said gently. 'You deserve no less.'

The words struck him, a soft but undeniable truth, settling deep within him. Why was he typically so generous with others yet so hard, so demanding, when it came to himself?

With a sigh, Andrew made a quiet but resolute commitment: to bridge the gap within himself, to close the divide between the care, the love, the honesty he gave to others and that which he withheld from himself. It wouldn't be easy, but in that moment, he knew it was necessary. The first step towards becoming whole.

Santi turned to the path ahead, his tone purposeful. 'Are you ready for the next step?'

Andrew followed with resolve, his mind clear. 'Yes, I am.'

15

Talents

Andrew and Santi moved steadily up the mountain trail, the soft, uneven earth crunching beneath their boots. The air was cooler here and thinner, but each step felt lighter, as though Andrew was being carried forwards by more than just his legs. After a while, he felt sufficiently at ease, both with the progress they were making and with the sense of companionship he felt with Santi, emboldening him to raise something that had been on his mind for some time.

'Forgive me for prying, Santi, but for all your wisdom and outward calm, I'm occasionally aware of a deep sadness in you. Why is that – or am I mistaken?'

Santi sighed. 'You are a very perceptive and sensitive young man. It's true... there's a raw, hollowed-out space inside me that I've been unable to fill. I lost someone very dear to me several years ago. Not a death but rather... an *estrangement*. But an estrangement that almost broke me.'

Amid his pity for the kindly old man, Andrew was curious. Who could Santi be referring to... a wife... a lover... a sibling... a child? But it didn't feel right to press him further.

'Forgive me if I don't share any more, my boy, but it's been hard for me to bear.' He grasped his staff in his right hand

and turned to face the mountain. 'Come. Let's make some distance while the sun is still high in the sky.'

Santi walked slightly ahead before slowing and falling into step beside him. He gestured towards the trees that stretched endlessly skywards. 'Do you notice how effortlessly nature thrives, Andrew? The trees grow, the rivers flow, the creatures move – none of them second-guessing their purpose. They don't resist their nature.'

Andrew followed the trail of a bee as it darted between flowers, gathering nectar with precise efficiency. 'Yes,' he murmured, a strange sense of calm settling over him. 'It's all so… natural. Everything just *is*. There's no force, no struggle. Everything moves with its own rhythm.'

Santi continued to look at the path ahead, but his voice held purpose. 'Let's talk about that rhythm within you – your transformational energy. Do you remember what that is?'

Andrew nodded slowly. 'My talents.'

'Exactly so. Tell me, Andrew…' Santi cast him a thoughtful glance. 'What do you believe a talent is?'

Andrew considered the question, his mind flashing to moments in his career when things had clicked effortlessly, to those rare times when he had been fully in the flow. 'A talent is… something we're naturally good at. Something that feels easy, even when others might find it difficult.'

Santi smiled, his eyes twinkling with quiet encouragement. 'Yes. Talents are gifts that don't involve force or struggle. They emerge naturally, like the way leaves convert light energy into chemical energy that feeds the tree while generating oxygen. But many people, even high achievers like you, miss something important.'

Andrew raised an eyebrow. 'What's that?'

'Talents aren't learned, Andrew. They're uncovered. They've been with you all along, waiting to be discovered and nurtured. The question is… have you uncovered yours?'

Andrew's steps slowed as he thought back over his life – his successes, his hard-fought achievements. But talents? Had he ever stopped to think what came naturally to him? Or had he been too caught up in proving himself to even notice? His shoulders tensed slightly. 'I'm not sure,' he admitted quietly.

Santi stopped beneath a towering spruce tree, its needles glistening in the soft sunlight. 'Let's uncover them together.' Wrapping both hands around the top of his staff, he looked at Andrew intently. 'There are two ways to unveil your core talents.'

Andrew tilted his head, listening attentively.

'The first is to look back to your childhood – before the world placed its expectations on you. What did you do effortlessly and enjoy? What made others marvel, even when you didn't understand why?'

'And the second?' Andrew asked.

'Imagine everyone who knows you best – family, friends, colleagues – all gathered in one room. Picture them discussing you. What would they say are your unique gifts? What you bring to the world that no one else does quite like you?

'Now, close your eyes. Take three deep breaths and invite your heart to reveal your three greatest talents. Don't search for them. Let them rise naturally.'

THE TREE AND THE MOUNTAIN

Andrew closed his eyes again as the cool mountain breeze brushed against his face. He inhaled deeply and slowly and his mind began to quieten. The sounds of the forest faded into the background, replaced by the gentle whisper of his breath.

Memories of childhood summers flickered into life – how he had loved solving puzzles, connecting random ideas and creating adventure stories as he ran through forests. They were joyous moments. He was just being himself...

Then the vision of a room appeared. He saw faces, heard their voices blending into a harmonious murmur. His wife, Lena, was sitting next to his mother. His children, Oliver and Audrey, were giggling on the couch. His mentor, Vijay, was nodding thoughtfully. Pete, his outspoken university friend, was gesturing animatedly. They were all talking about him. Words floated through the air, circling him like leaves caught on a breeze. And then, like pieces of a puzzle clicking into place, the voices became clear.

Andrew opened his eyes, the forest coming back into focus around him. 'I've got them,' he said softly.

Santi's gaze held firm. 'What did you find?'

Andrew's chest rose and fell as he spoke. '*Connecting the dots... powerful communication... empathy.*'

Santi smiled faintly. 'Tell me about them.'

Andrew composed himself. 'Connecting the dots... I've always done that. Whether it's piecing together ideas or understanding people, I can see patterns where others see chaos. It's like I can build bridges between things that seem disconnected.'

'Powerful communication?'

'I've always had a way with words – written or spoken. Whether in law or personal conversations, I can make people understand and feel things. It's not just about talking; it's about creating meaning.'

Santi leaned forwards on his staff. 'And empathy?'

Andrew hesitated at first. 'I feel what others feel. I can sense their emotions, even when they try to hide them. It's why people trust me. But it's also overwhelming at times.'

Santi's smile radiated warmth and wisdom. 'These talents, Andrew, are the way you alter the world around you. They are your transformational energy, flowing naturally and effortlessly outwards, simply by the fact of being *you*, enriching the lives of others in the process. Like a tree photosynthesising or a bee pollinating, your talents have the power to nourish others – and to fuel your own growth.'

The words sank deep into Andrew's core.

'When you use them freely, consciously, you enter a natural state of low effort, high enjoyment and high output.'

Andrew's heart swelled with quiet determination. He had spent so much of his life sacrificing, believing that success required a heavy price. But what if there was another way? A different way? One that didn't drain him but elevated him?

The two companions resumed their climb together, the path becoming less distinct as the slope steepened.

With each step, Andrew felt himself drawing closer to something greater – not just the mountain's peak, but the version of himself he was meant to be.

16

Aspirations

Andrew and Santi climbed higher, the mountain trail narrowing as jagged rocks jutted from the earth like forgotten bones. The crunch of scree beneath their boots and the occasional rustle of leaves filled the stillness.

Santi waved his staff at the towering trees that stretched endlessly into the sky. 'Do you see how they grow, Andrew? Their branches reach upwards, always seeking the light. That's what aspirations do for us. They pull us towards what we truly desire. But unlike these trees, we often lose the ability to listen to that pull.'

'Why is that?' Andrew said.

'Probably because we allow ourselves to be sucked into a reactionary, short-term mode of what is immediately in front of us.'

Andrew nodded, his mind drifting towards his daily routine of putting out fires in other people's lives.

Santi brought him back to the present. 'Are you ready to rediscover your aspirations?'

Andrew didn't answer immediately. He looked up at the mountain's distant peak veiled in mist. Its vastness stirred both awe and unease, its silence pressing unspoken questions into his mind as he pondered a life spent chasing without understanding. 'I think I am,' he said finally, though his doubts were undeniable.

'What do you believe aspirations are?' Santi said.

Andrew searched for an answer, his thoughts swirling like the shifting winds around them. 'They're... what we aim for,' he said slowly. 'Giving us direction.'

'Direction...' Santi let the word linger in the air like the fading echo of a bell. 'Without it, we can spend our lives chasing shadows, mistaking effort for purpose and motion for progress.'

Mistaking effort for purpose and motion for progress...

The truth of those words struck Andrew deep in his core. He thought about his life... every long night, every success that never seemed enough... the relentless pursuit of a future that always felt just out of reach.

Santi planted his staff into the earth, calling Andrew to a halt. 'Let's try something that will invite purpose and direction, shall we? Imagine you hold Aladdin's lamp inside your heart and you're granted three wishes. And the three wishes you have relate to these three questions...

'Who do you want to *be*?

'What do you want to *do*?

'What do you want to *have*?'

Andrew blinked, the simplicity of the exercise disarming him. He closed his eyes and placed his hands over his chest. But instead of calmness, a storm of competing desires swirled wildly within him. His ambitions, regrets, distractions all clamoured for attention. Frustration welled up inside him and his eyes popped open. 'I don't know,' he confessed, his voice heavy. 'There's too much noise.'

'Then breathe,' Santi instructed. 'Let the noise settle. Take six deep breaths. Trust that your heart will speak to you.'

Andrew shut his eyes again reluctantly, but as he inhaled deeply, five seconds in and five seconds out, the storm inside him began to calm. The noise faded, like ripples on a lake slowly dissipating. With each breath, a stillness spread through him and he felt something stir within.

'Now,' Santi's voice whispered through the quiet. 'Who do you want to *be*?'

Andrew's mind stilled and behind his closed eyes, an image emerged. He saw himself laughing with his children, his arms wrapped around his wife, his face free of tension. He wasn't trying to prove himself nor burdened with expectations. He was simply there, fully present, fully himself. A warmth spread through his chest as the realisation bloomed.

'I want to be free,' he whispered. 'To be myself.'

Santi let the image settle before he asked, 'What do you want to *do*?'

This time, the answer came more easily. He saw himself sharing stories, connecting with people, travelling not for business but for discovery and meaning. He saw a life of purpose rooted not in accomplishment but in connection.

Finally, came the third question: 'What do you want to *have*?'

The answer was immediate: *Time*. Time to savour life with his family, time to explore his passions, time to just *be*.

Andrew opened his eyes, exhaling slowly. The mountain air felt warmer now, as though the sunlight had softened just for him.

Santi studied him with a knowing smile. 'What did you uncover?'

Andrew's tone was assured, his words resonating with newfound conviction. 'My BE aspiration is to be *my true self*... happy, confident, and free. My DO aspiration is to *inspire and connect* through stories and experiences. And my HAVE aspiration is to have *time* – to live fully, with my family and for myself.'

Santi nodded and smiled broadly. 'Few people pause to ask themselves these questions, Andrew. That's why life often feels unplanned, even accidental. But when you define your aspirations, you gain something rare and powerful... *clarity*. A clear vision of who you want to be and the life you want to live. Those who truly understand their aspirations don't just wait for destiny – they create it. Because they know what they truly want.'

Andrew closed his eyes, letting his aspirations sink in – not as distant wishes but as something real, something alive. They had always been there, waiting beneath the noise of daily life, ready to be found.

Santi broke the silence, his voice thoughtful. 'This clarity is the antidote to the uncertainty the world throws at us every day.'

Andrew's eyes opened and, in that instant, something clicked. A shift, a realisation, not just in thought, but in feeling.

ASPIRATIONS

Clarity...
Of his *values.*
Of his *talents.*
Of his *aspirations.*
Of *who he was* and *who he wanted to become.*

For the first time, he wasn't looking outwards for direction. The answers weren't in the world around him; they were within. And clarity wasn't about certainty or control – it was about seeing himself, trusting himself and knowing his path was his to create.

As if sensing the transformation, Santi said nothing at first. Instead, he laid a hand on Andrew's shoulder – a simple gesture, but one that carried warmth, recognition and quiet understanding. 'Well done, Andrew. You're fully connecting with yourself. Now, are you ready to take the next steps?'

Andrew's smile broadened and his chest filled with something light yet powerful. 'Absolutely!' he said with exuberance.

As they continued up the trail, the summit felt closer than ever – not just a peak to conquer but a marker of something far greater. A milestone in his becoming.

17

The Power of Nine

The mountain path steepened as Andrew and Santi climbed higher, the uneven terrain demanding careful footing with every step. Andrew's breathing synced effortlessly with the rhythm of the climb. The thinning canopy revealed glimpses of the sprawling valley below, bathed in golden light, while the cool, crisp air at altitude cleansed his thoughts as it filled his lungs.

Andrew felt different – lighter, yet firmly anchored. A calming energy pulsed through him, not the fleeting adrenaline he had known in the past but something deeper, quieter and infinitely stronger.

Santi walked beside him, his steps deliberate and sure. As they reached a clearing, he turned to Andrew, his eyes calm yet searching. 'How are you feeling?'

Andrew halted and looked out across the forested expanse below that stretched towards the endless horizon. He drew a long breath, savouring the clarity that had been building within him. 'I feel… energised. Like I'm capable of anything.'

Santi's faint smile flickered. 'That's the energy of your Power of Nine awakening within you.'

Andrew tilted his head, intrigued. 'Power of Nine?'

Santi led him further into the clearing. The space felt sacred, as though the mountain had carved it out specifically for them. He faced Andrew, his expression both warm and serious. 'Your Power of Nine is the alignment of the most vital forces within you. It's the energy that forms your central alignment line – the three core values that ground you, the three natural talents that drive you and the three aspirations that guide you. When you align these, you connect with your most authentic self, unlocking your true power.'

Andrew's thoughts raced, trying to weave Santi's words together. He visualised a vertical line running through him, from his feet to the crown of his head, connecting him to both the earth and the sky.

'How do I use this Power of Nine in my life?' Andrew asked, eagerly.

'I'll show you.' Santi placed his hands over his heart. 'Close your eyes,' he instructed softly. 'Imagine yourself on a ship, a grand and beautiful ship, sailing across the open sea. On its hull are inscribed your values, keeping it balanced and steady through every storm.'

Andrew followed Santi's guidance, placing his hands over his heart and closing his eyes, the vision of the ship taking shape. He saw the hull engraved with the words *Love... Honesty... Making a Difference*. The ship sliced through the waves effortlessly, its course true.

'Now, imagine its sails,' Santi continued. 'They're your talents billowing in the wind, propelling you forward.'

In his mind's eye, the sails swelled with power, the symbols of his talents, *Connecting the Dots... Powerful*

THE POWER OF NINE

Communication... Empathy, illuminating the canvas. The wind pushed the ship forwards so that it cut through the waves with precision.

'And at the helm,' Santi said, 'is you, the captain. Your hands are on the wheel, steering you towards your aspirations.'

Andrew imagined himself standing at the wheel, his grip firm, guiding the ship towards the horizon. The words *Be the Real Me... Do Good... Have Time...* were etched into the wood beneath his hands. He felt the vastness of the sea, its infinite possibilities stretching before him. Yet instead of fear he felt a strong resolve. He wasn't lost. He had a destination.

'Now open your eyes,' Santi said.

Andrew obeyed.

'How would you feel if you began every morning with that vision?'

Andrew smiled. Self-doubt was nowhere to be found. 'I'd feel unstoppable,' he said with quiet certainty.

Santi's eyes twinkled. 'But know this... life will try to knock you off course. It always does. Storms will roll in to test you. The key is to realign yourself when that happens. That's the power of your central alignment line. It's always there to guide you back to who you are.'

As they walked on in silence, Andrew set about absorbing the lessons he had learned.

After a short while, upon reaching a small plateau, Santi stopped. He turned to look at Andrew, his eyes filled with something deeper than pride... *trust*. 'This is where I leave you,' he said gently.

Andrew's chest tightened. 'You're leaving?'

'I've taken you as far as I can for now. The rest of the journey is yours to make. But remember… everything you need, you already carry within you.'

Andrew swallowed, emotion rising in his throat. 'Thank you,' he said, his voice filled with gratitude.

Santi crossed his hands over his heart and smiled, the warmth in his eyes like a father's parting blessing.

'Listen to your heart, Andrew. It is both wise and kind, and deserving of your trust. It will guide you home.'

With those final words, Santi turned and began his descent, his figure fading into the shadows of the setting sun.

18

The Lake

As Andrew left the clearing behind, his body moved with a new rhythm, a kind of effortless ease that surprised him. The wind picked up, brushing against his face and rustling the trees that lined the narrow trail.

His mind lingered on Santi's departure. The emptiness of his absence felt vast, a hollow space where wisdom and guidance had once been. How many people in his life had left impressions as indelible as Santi's? No one had shown him how to listen to the whispers of his own soul.

Santi had given him something priceless: an understanding of the energy within him, a way to connect with his values, talents and aspirations – the essence of his *nature*. The thought filled him with a quiet power. He felt alive in a way he hadn't for years.

After a while, he stopped to catch his breath, and for a moment, he allowed himself to truly see the world around him. The trees stood tall, their branches swaying gently as though rooted in the same moment he now inhabited. Nature wasn't rushing. It wasn't worrying about what came next. It was simply *being* – in the present, fully alive.

'Nature's clock,' Andrew murmured, a faint smile tugging at his lips.

THE TREE AND THE MOUNTAIN

The light was beginning to fade. Streaks of gold and orange spread across the sky like spilled ink bleeding into the horizon. The sun dipped lower, casting long shadows across the trees and bathing the landscape in a warm, ethereal glow. Andrew's thoughts drifted to practical concerns: how much further had he to climb and where might he rest for the night? He realised with a faint unease that he didn't have the answers.

The trail narrowed as it wound around a bend and his musings were interrupted by an unexpected sight. There, nestled between the trees, lay a mountain lake, its waters so still they mirrored the sky perfectly. The fiery colours of the sunset reflected on its surface, making it look like a portal into another world. Andrew gasped. It appeared untouched. Sacred.

He approached cautiously. The silence was profound, broken only by the faint rustling of spruce needles and the soft ripple of water as a single leaf drifted lazily across its surface. Kneeling by the edge, he leaned forwards and saw his reflection staring back at him.

His face looked… different. The lines of tension to which he had grown so accustomed were softer, and the dark patches he usually had beneath his eyes seemed lighter. He tilted his head, studying his reflection as if he were seeing himself for the first time. Was it the light, or had something within him truly changed?

Tentatively, he reached down and dipped his fingers into the water. The icy shock travelled up his arm, making him gasp. The cold was invigorating, like a lightning bolt to his

THE LAKE

senses. Cupping a handful of water, he splashed it onto his face. The droplets clung to his skin before sliding down his cheeks, grounding him fully in the moment.

He stood up and walked along the edge of the lake, his footsteps muffled by the soft earth. Each step revealed something new: wildflowers glowing in the fading light, their delicate petals trembling in the breeze; moss-covered rocks scattered like forgotten relics; the gentle trickle of a stream that spilled over the edge of the lake.

Then, something across the water caught his eye. Andrew froze. On the far shore, someone was crouching by the edge of the lake, silhouetted against the fading glow of the sky. They moved with purpose, gathering something from the ground.

Curiosity quickened Andrew's pace as he continued to follow the curve of the lake. His mind raced with questions: *Who is it? Why are they here?*

As he drew closer, he cleared his throat, announcing his presence. The figure straightened and turned, their eyes meeting his. For a brief moment, the world seemed to hold its breath. The woman was wearing a pair of dungarees cinched in at the waist with a brown leather belt and her dark hair was held in a loose braid that fell across her shoulder. In her arms, she bore an enormous bundle of kindling and yet, somehow, she seemed to balance her burden effortlessly.

Despite the simplicity of her clothes, her face had a stark, regal quality. She wasn't at all like Lena, whose soft, dark curls, heart-shaped face and liquid brown eyes had stolen his heart right from the start. This face bore more resemblance

to the Greek statues of Athena or perhaps the portraits of a young Queen Elizabeth I. There was also a hint of weariness about her, as if she'd had to bear too much on her shoulders for too long. Nevertheless, her piercing eyes scanned him quickly, as if assessing every detail.

'About time you showed up!' She was brisk, confident and commanding.

Andrew blinked, thrown by her unexpected familiarity and feeling somewhat affronted. 'Excuse me?'

She smirked, shifting the heavy kindling in her arms. 'Santi said you'd be here eventually.'

Andrew's heart thudded in his chest, a mix of confusion and anticipation flooding through him. 'You're a friend of Santi?' He took a step closer.

'An associate. We used to be very close.' The woman looked wistful for a moment, her expression softening slightly. 'But then someone pushed us apart.'

Andrew studied the woman. The two of them clearly shared a secret he had yet to uncover.

'Anyway, I'm here to help you finish what he started.'

Andrew sighed. The significance of the moment rang out like the final note of a symphony. The mountain had one more lesson to teach him, and it seemed this woman was about to deliver it.

19

The Truth

The woman huffed impatiently, tossing a bundle of kindling onto a growing pile. 'Night's falling,' she said. 'Start gathering more branches.' Her tone left no room for argument.

As if on cue, a distant howl, primitive and bestial, echoed from woods further up the mountain, chilling Andrew's blood. Then came another... and another. 'Wolves?'

'Don't worry about those. They can't harm us... at least not yet...'

Andrew bent down to gather wood, his mind in a spin. As he laid the branches beside her, he ventured cautiously, 'You were expecting me.'

'Yes,' she replied curtly, not even sparing him a glance. 'And you're late.'

Andrew's confusion deepened. 'Late for what?'

Straightening up, she met his gaze with a sharp intensity. 'Late to help me and late on your journey.' Her voice was as crisp as the mountain air. 'You've been enjoying your climb, haven't you? But how much time do you think you have left?'

The question struck Andrew like a punch to the chest. Recalling Santi's estimate, he had around eighteen hours at best, and for half of those it would be dark. His mind filled with images of Lena's warm smile, Oliver's and Audrey's laughter. The familiar ache of missing them was joined by something sharper – *panic!*

'What exactly are we doing?' he asked, his voice tight. 'Can you help me up the mountain? I need to get there immediately.'

The woman continued piling up wood, her movements brisk and efficient. 'Yes and yes,' she said, without missing a beat. 'But first we must build a shelter. The nights here are cold, and you'll need your strength for the final climb tomorrow morning.'

Andrew fell into step beside her, working quickly as the fading light painted the landscape amber and gold. His questions didn't stop swirling, but her composure comforted him. As they finished the shelter, a simple but sturdy structure that felt solid against the encroaching night, his curiosity finally boiled over.

'What's your name?' he asked. 'And how did you get here?'

She sat down on a flat stone, wiping her hands on her dungarees before answering. 'Sophia,' she said, simply. 'But the real question is who are *you* and how did *you* get here?' Her gaze locked onto his, piercing and unrelenting.

It felt as if she were peeling back layers of him, exposing truths he had worked hard to keep hidden. He exhaled slowly, the exhaustion of keeping up appearances settling over him. 'Do you want me to tell you my story?'

'I want the *truth*,' she answered, emphatically.

'I'm a lawyer,' he began, the words feeling heavier than usual. 'But lately, it's felt more like I'm a firefighter in a suit.

THE TRUTH

The pressure never stops. I'm always on edge, even when I'm supposed to be relaxing.'

Sophia's expression softened slightly, her silence coaxing him to continue.

'I keep pushing because I'm terrified that, if I don't, everything will fall apart. I give everything I have at work, but by the time I come home, I'm spent. I have nothing left to give to the people I love most. They get the leftovers.' His voice faltered as memories of his family filled his mind: Oliver and Audrey running to hug him… Lena watching quietly and hoping he'd be fully present for once.

'I've done everything I thought I was supposed to do,' he said, his voice breaking slightly. 'Worked hard, climbed the ladder, made partner. But instead of feeling fulfilled, I have a huge void inside me. I've been running so fast and for so long, I don't even know what I'm running towards anymore.'

Suddenly all his frustrations spilled over. 'It's not right. I don't deserve this. I've done everything expected of me. I've worked hard, had a successful career and been a good provider for my family. Things should be better.'

'A good provider? Give me strength! Is that what you think your family needs from you? Were you asleep when you spent time with Santi?'

'That's unfair!' Andrew protested. 'And he taught me a lot. He was patient, kind and insightful – not a bit like someone else I could think of.'

'Ah, you want insightful?' Sophia narrowed her eyes. 'All right, Andrew… what's the last thing your wife said to you? Do you even remember?'

Andrew thought for a moment. He realised Lena said pretty much the same thing every morning. 'See you when you land,' he said.

'Really?' said Sophia. 'And is that what she used to say in the early years of your marriage?'

He cast his mind back to a time before Oliver and Audrey were born, when he was still establishing himself at the law firm. 'Back then, she'd ask me when I expected to be home. Now she's a lot more settled.'

'Settled?' Sophia scowled. 'She's not settled, Andrew, she's *resigned*. Resigned the way your mother had become before the break-up with your father.'

Andrew recoiled as if he'd just been slapped.

A long silence stretched between them as Sophia fed the fire, glancing over at him occasionally. He wrestled with the crushing realisation that, back in the world he'd left behind, his marriage had been slowly but relentlessly moving towards a precipice and that the tragedy that had befallen his parents had every possibility of being repeated. He wasn't willing to lose Lena – his love, his rock – nor would he allow Oliver and Audrey to go through the disruption and loneliness he and his brother had suffered. Getting back to his own world, to his life as he knew it, remained an imperative, but it was no longer enough. However abrupt Sophia might be, there was no denying her perceptiveness or her good intentions, and he needed all the help he could get.

'How could I be so blind?' he said. 'I always chased the next thing – the next challenge.' His confession spilled from him like water from a broken dam. 'But I've rarely chosen a path for myself. I've followed the paths that others think are worthwhile. And now… despite having what appears to be everything, I feel lost and in danger of losing everything of value to me.'

'Don't I know it,' Sophia said. 'I often feel lost too – and so tired. For the last ten years, I've had to take on more and more of a burden than ever before. Too often I've had to toil alone, overcoming a lack of guidance – get by without a map or compass, unsure of my own purpose.'

'Forgive me,' Andrew said, 'but I don't see how that has anything to do with me.'

'It has more to do with you than you could possibly imagine,' she said. 'Now, tell me… what is it you're truly seeking on this mountain?'

Andrew's breath hitched. The answer wasn't easy, but he searched for it, peeling back the noise until only truth remained. 'I want to be reunited with my family,' he said quietly. 'But I also want to be *myself* again. I want to walk a path that feels right for me – and for them.'

A genuine smile spread across Sophia's face, warming the cool night air. 'Then we have work to do. To begin, we need to focus on one of the most powerful forces within you, the one that shapes how you see the world and navigate your life.'

Andrew leaned in slightly, his curiosity rekindled. 'What is it?'

Sophia's eyes glimmered in the fading light. When she spoke, her voice was charged with meaning.

'Your mind.'

20

The Mind

The rising moon cast its soft glow across the lake like a watchful guardian. The air felt sacred, as if the mountain itself was holding its breath, waiting for a revelation.

Andrew stole a glance at Sophia, who was sitting cross-legged beside him, her face serene, albeit with a trace of weariness, her eyes fixed on the orb above them.

Finally, she tilted her head and spoke. 'Tell me, Andrew… what do you really know about your mind?'

He shifted slightly, his fingers brushing the cool, damp earth. 'I guess… I've never thought about it deeply,' he admitted. 'It's an operating system, right? Something that keeps everything running.'

Sophia leaned forwards, her eyes meeting his, piercing but now kinder. 'It's much more than that.' Her voice was deliberate, like the first note of a song. 'Your mind is a supercomputer, one of the most powerful systems ever designed. It plans, solves problems, makes decisions. But do you know how it does all that?'

Andrew frowned slightly, thinking back to years of mental exertion, late nights and endless decisions. 'I suppose its drive is to keep me productive. Performing. Pushing forward.'

Sophia's smile was subtle, *meaningful*. 'Absolutely so. The mind is focused on performance. From the moment you wake up in the morning to the moment you fall asleep at night, it is doing everything it can to keep you alive and productive. But let me ask you this... do you feel that constant drive, like a continuous hum in the background, even when you try to rest?'

Andrew inhaled sharply. The truth of her words struck a chord deep within him. He thought of the late nights when his mind refused to quieten down... the endless lists... the nagging thought that he hadn't done enough. 'Yes,' he said quietly. 'It never stops.'

Sophia's gaze didn't waver. 'And when you *do* achieve something – when you finally reach the goal you've been chasing – does it bring you peace?'

Andrew's fingers curled into the soil beneath him. He thought of the promotions, the accolades, the milestones he had celebrated briefly before moving on to the next. 'No,' he whispered. 'There's always something else. Something more to achieve.'

The silence that followed was profound, like the pause between heartbeats.

Sophia broke the stillness. 'Here's the thing... there's nothing wrong with your mind. In fact, it's brilliant – doing exactly what it was designed to do. Keeping you alive... pushing you to achieve. But the problem...' Her tone grew firmer. '...is when you let it take over.'

Andrew looked up, confusion flickering across his face. 'Take over?'

THE MIND

'Your mind makes for an excellent employee but a terrible boss.'

Andrew sat back as her words sank in. They were so true. He thought of the sleepless nights, the constant striving, the exhaustion that never seemed to lift.

'It's great at solving problems and executing tasks, but when it's in charge it pushes you beyond your limits – towards exhaustion, burnout and disconnection. It doesn't know how to stop. That's why you never have enough time. It's always moving the goalpost.'

'But how do I stop it?' The desperation in his own voice cut through the night air. 'How do I make it step down?'

Sophia raised her eyebrows a little. 'You change boss.'

Andrew blinked, the simplicity of the statement throwing him off balance. 'Change boss?'

She nodded. 'The mind isn't meant to lead. The real boss, the one that should guide you, is something else.'

Andrew's stomach lurched, a flicker of recognition sparking inside him. 'The heart!' he said, almost in disbelief. Unbidden came the image of an old man with a staff sitting by an oak tree.

Sophia's smile widened, her eyes gleaming in the firelight. 'Bravo,' she whispered, her voice carrying on the wind like a sacred truth. 'Your heart is the leader. It knows what truly matters... your family... your wellbeing... your purpose. When the heart leads, the mind follows. It listens and executes the heart's priorities, not its own. That's when balance is restored.'

Andrew's breathing became slower, deeper. For so long, he had buried his heart beneath layers of logic, ambition and endless tasks. Now, he could feel it stirring, emerging from its cocoon.

'What happens when the heart leads?' he said, his voice quiet. He needed to know more.

Sophia's gaze softened further, her tone a whisper of reassurance. 'It guides us towards our ultimate purpose.'

Andrew's eyes met hers, searching. 'And what's that?'

'The purpose of being *you*. Not the version you think you need to be for others, but the *real* you.'

The words struck him deeply, dislodging years of chasing external validation. *The purpose of being me.* It wasn't about achieving more, proving himself or ticking off accomplishments. It was about rediscovering who he was beneath it all – his values… his dreams… his essence. After a long, contemplative silence, he asked, 'What happens when the heart and mind work together?'

Sophia smiled. Raising her hands, she held her two index fingers side by side. 'When they align,' she said with a playful twinkle, 'one plus one doesn't equal two. It equals eleven.'

Andrew chuckled softly, Sophia's child-like explanation filling him with warmth.

He knew the summit lay in wait up ahead. He felt ready. His heart would lead the way, and his mind would follow. Together, an unstoppable force. He closed his eyes for a moment, breathing deeply. 'Together…' he whispered, as darkness fell.

21

Decisions

Above them, the stars glittered like lanterns scattered across a velvet sky. For the first time in years, Andrew felt their glow within him, as though he were aligning with something greater.

Sophia rose gracefully and inspected the shelter they had built with quiet precision. Her movements were calm and confident, the actions of someone who always knew the next step before taking it. Satisfied, she turned to him, her expression warm but focused. 'Shall we make some dinner?'

His stomach answered before he could. The knot of hunger he hadn't hitherto acknowledged tightened at the thought of food.

Sophia gestured to a basket filled with impossibly fresh produce. 'Vegetables OK?'

'Perfect,' said Andrew.

She handed him a matchbox and looked over at the fire pit. 'Why don't you get the fire going while I prepare the food?'

Andrew smiled faintly, memories of campfire evenings flashing through his mind. He collected some dry twigs and leaves and created a tepee out of them with practised care. With a few strikes of a match, the fire sputtered into life. Crouching low to the ground, he gently coaxed the flames, feeding them gradually until they burned steadily and cast flickering shadows across their encampment.

'Nicely done,' Sophia said, as she approached. Soon, she was slicing into an eggplant atop a rough slab of bark she had transformed into a makeshift chopping board. Her movements were so methodical and efficient.

Andrew sat down beside her, the warmth of the fire radiating into his back. His curiosity was stirring again. 'Sophia, earlier you talked about aligning the heart and the mind. How does that work in practice? Especially when you're called on to make decisions?'

Sophia looked up from her slicing, a spark of intrigue illuminating her eyes. 'The quality of our decisions has a direct influence on the quality of our lives. Yet how often do we actually consider *how* we make them?'

Andrew tilted his head. 'Not enough, I imagine.'

Sophia smiled. 'We're taught *what* to decide – what's practical, what's expected – but not *how* to decide in a way that truly serves us. And that's why so many people feel lost, making choices that leave them empty.'

Andrew's mind raced. He thought of the countless decisions he'd made under pressure, reacting to external demands without pausing to reflect. 'So, how does one make better decisions?'

Sophia set down the sliced eggplant and met his gaze. 'By using a process. One of which we are conscious… where we understand its steps. That's what gives us the confidence to make decisions and not regret them.'

'What can that look like?'

DECISIONS

She examined a slice of eggplant as if it held a hidden lesson. A smile unfurled across her face. 'Let's use preparing our meal as a metaphor for how to create a decision-making process.'

Andrew leaned in as she picked up a whole eggplant.

'Let's start with the first step... *information*. Imagine this eggplant represents the information you need to make a good decision. Ask yourself:

'First, what relevant information do I already have?' She made the first slice.

'Second, what critical information am I missing?' *Slice.*

'Third, where can I find that missing information?' *Slice.*

As the slices piled up neatly on the bark, Andrew thought back to moments when he had acted on incomplete information, driven by urgency rather than clarity.

Sophia reached into the basket for a ripe tomato, its skin glistening in the firelight. 'Now, let's bring in external perspectives. These represent the people and resources that can help you see what you might not. Ask yourself:

'First, who are the three people I trust most to give me honest feedback or advice?' She halved the tomato.

'Second, what other reliable sources can I consult?' *Chop.*

'Third, how can they help me avoid any blind spots?' *Chop.*

Andrew imagined conversations with trusted mentors and friends, visualising how their insights could have changed some of his past decisions. How often he had either ignored their advice or asked too late.

Sophia reached into the basket again, this time pulling out three field mushrooms. 'Now we turn inwards.' She cupped the mushrooms in her palm. 'Your mind, your gut and your heart… all three have something to say. To hear them, ask:

'First, what is my mind recommending?' She cut the first mushroom in two.

'Second, what is my gut warning me about?' *Cut.*

'Third, what is my heart whispering to me?' *Cut.*

Andrew flinched slightly at the last question. He wasn't sure he had ever truly listened to his heart when making decisions. The whisper had always been drowned out by logic, deadlines and the expectations of others.

Sophia put the mushrooms aside and picked up an onion. 'Finally, the most important filter… alignment with who you are. Ask yourself:

'First, does this option align with my values?' She peeled away a layer of the onion.

'Second, does it allow me to use my talents?' *Peel.*

'Third, does it bring me closer to my aspirations?' *Peel.*

As the sharp scent of onion filled the air, Andrew blinked, his thoughts falling into place. *Consult my Power of Nine! Of course!* How revealing and useful that would be.

He pictured decisions from his past, times when he had chosen paths that didn't align with his core values or which had pushed him further away from what truly mattered. They had never ended well.

Sophia gathered together the vegetables and dropped them into a pan over the fire. Soon, the food was sizzling, filling the air with a rich, smoky aroma that made Andrew's stomach growl again. 'When you have a structured process for decision-making,' Sophia continued, stirring the pan,

'you don't just react... you respond. Your decisions come from clarity and alignment, not from fear or pressure.'

She served him a plate of stir-fried vegetables, their vibrant colours glowing in the firelight. '*Voilà, monsieur,*' she said playfully, handing it to him.

Andrew took a mouthful, savouring the flavours. But more nourishing than the food were her words and the clarity they brought. He thought of the journey ahead – not just of the climb to the summit but of the choices waiting for him along the way. With every decision, he could now exercise a clear process, with his heart, mind and gut working together.

The fire crackled, its warmth seeping into his skin as the stars above flickered like distant torches lighting the way. He felt at peace – not because he had all the answers but because he finally had a compass to help him find them.

22

Sensitivity

Shadows danced on the tall pines and the night settled in with a gentle stillness. Looking into the fire, Andrew sat back, his eyes tracing the curve of the flames as they licked upwards, reaching for the heavens. Sophia sat across from him, illuminated by the firelight. She was quiet, her presence calm and measured, as though she were giving him space to find his footing. In response to Sophia's wisdom, Andrew felt inclined to share a maxim of his own.

'One of the most useful things somebody once taught me was never to do today's work tomorrow,' he said. 'It's something that's helped me immeasurably.'

'Impressive,' Sophia said. 'Does this *seize the day* mantra only function within the sacred hallows of Visconti, Kellermann & Partners or does it also work for tree houses?'

Andrew was baffled for a moment. 'I'm not sure I—'

'Didn't you once promise yourself that you'd build a tree house for your children? When did you expect to do it?'

'I thought I'd wait until Oliver was seven and Audrey was five.'

'And?'

Andrew's face fell. It was coming up to Oliver's ninth birthday. 'I've been distracted…' he said, lamely.

'You earn enough,' Sophia said. 'You could have paid someone to install a tree house.'

'No,' he said. 'I won't do that. It's not the same.'

Sophia smiled broadly, almost as if in relief. 'You still have it in you to reconcile your mind with your heart, Andrew, that much is clear.'

Andrew smiled back at her. 'A tree house today, not tomorrow – at least assuming I can get home. Yet another reason why I must return. I'll take any help you can give me.'

'Ask away,' she said.

Taking a moment, he turned away from the flames and looked out across the lake's shimmering surface. Finally, he spoke. 'Why do I always feel like something's missing?'

'What do you mean?'

'I mean, there seems to be a missing part of the puzzle within me, a void that's always been there regardless of what I do or say. It never seems to go away.'

Sophia nodded, thoughtfully. 'The question often holds the answer,' she said, her tone soft but deliberate, like the rustling of leaves before a storm.

Why do I always feel like something's missing? Andrew repeated to himself.

'Tell me, Andrew… when was the last time you let yourself truly *feel*? Not think, but *feel* what's within you and around you, letting your sensitivity fully express itself?'

Andrew frowned. *Sensitivity?* It had always been something to suppress, a vulnerability he couldn't afford in his fast-paced, high-achieving world.

'I don't think I ever have,' he admitted, his voice heavy with honesty. 'Sensitivity always seemed… impractical. Something you put away when there's work to be done. My father is a good man – a good father, in fact, though something of an old-school stoic. And I think that after he and my mother separated, and he knew he wouldn't be around so much, he wanted me and my brother to be strong. I think he may have planted a notion within me that associates sensitivity with weakness.'

'That's the trap many fall into,' Sophia said gently. 'High achievers like you lean so heavily on intellect and precision that sensitivity gets buried. But that doesn't mean it's gone. It's waiting, Andrew. And it holds the key to something far more powerful than just solving problems or reaching goals.'

Andrew listened, but scepticism flickered within him. He had built his career and life on logic, analysis and clear thinking. 'The key to what?'

Sophia turned to the lake, its surface glinting with the reflection of the moon. 'Look at the water,' she said softly. 'It reflects the world above… the trees, the sky, the stars. But beneath the surface there's an entire ecosystem of life… fish… plants… currents. Mysteries that most people never notice.'

Andrew followed her gaze, the stillness of the lake drawing him in.

'Your sensitivity is like the depths of the lake. It's always been there, shaping how you experience life, even if you haven't paid any attention to it. It's what allows you to sense what isn't obvious – emotions left unspoken… opportunities disguised as problems… the undercurrents guiding you.

That's where your intuition lives. And intuition is a superpower, an internal compass directing you to what *feels* right, not just what appears logical.'

Andrew's chest tightened as memories surfaced: moments when he had felt an inexplicable pull or sense of knowing, only to dismiss it as coincidence. How many times had he ignored that voice in favour of cold, calculated reasoning?

'How do I access that part of myself?' His voice was quieter now, almost reverent.

Sophia turned to him, her eyes reflecting the firelight. 'You already are. The fact that you're asking is the first step. Sensitivity is about noticing – how you feel... how others make you feel... how the world around you feels. Once you start noticing, you'll begin to access what's beneath the surface. And from there, that insight leads to foresight. That's how wisdom is born.'

Insight, leading to foresight, leading to wisdom...

The fire crackled again and Andrew felt the air shift. The cool breeze brushed past him, sharper now, carrying the scent of pine with greater intensity. Even the rustling leaves seemed more vivid, as though he were tuning into a frequency that he hadn't realised existed, a language he was only beginning to understand.

'You've spent years training your intellect,' Sophia said. 'But your sensitivity will take you deeper and further. It's where you'll make decisions, not just from thought but from a place of *knowing* – a knowing that doesn't need proof or validation.'

THE TREE AND THE MOUNTAIN

Knowing without knowing... The idea settled in Andrew like yet another piece of a puzzle sliding into place. He stared into the flames, their flickering shapes curling upwards as if they too were reaching for something unseen. His breathing slowed and wonder tinged his voice as he asked, 'What would happen if I learned to embrace this part of myself?'

Sophia's lips curved into a warm smile. 'You would connect to your deep intuitive state, a place accessible only when your heart and mind work in unison. It's not about forcing decisions or overthinking them. It's about allowing them to flow naturally because you're connected to something deeper. That's when choices aren't just made – they're felt and embodied. It's also the moment you stop chasing the *right place* and start living in the right *space*.'

'Can you elaborate?'

Sophia's gaze held his, composed and patient. 'Searching for the right place is an external pursuit. The unspoken belief is that if we find the right job, the right relationship, the right opportunity, everything will click and we'll finally feel fulfilled. But that's an illusion.'

She leaned back, letting her words settle. 'The truth is, when you live in the right space *internally*, when your intellect and sensitivity are in harmony, you create the conditions for the right place to find you. For the right person to find you. The right opportunity. You no longer need to chase them. You naturally give off the energy that draws them to you. It's not magic... it's resonance.'

Andrew's pulse quickened as her words sank in. Throughout his life he had always been chasing – the next goal, the next promotion, the next milestone – always convinced that success lay just beyond the horizon. It had taken him far. But what if the key to him being successful and not losing himself on the journey wasn't *out there*? What if it was inside him, waiting for him to notice and tune in?

He met Sophia's gaze, and she smiled softly, as though she could already sense the shift taking place within him.

'So,' Andrew said, his voice steady, 'the key isn't just to search for the right place. It's to cultivate the right space inside myself and trust that the outside will follow naturally – be it a life partner, a job, a place to live.'

Sophia smiled. 'That's right. Let your heart guide, your mind execute and your energy speak. You will attract the right opportunities and the right people into your life. Your truth will speak to the universe and it will answer.'

Giddy excitement washed over Andrew, not just from her words but from an emerging potential. Deep within, he sensed a burgeoning connection to something far greater than any destination he had ever pursued.

23

Internal Narratives

Sitting cross-legged by the fire, Andrew watched the flickering flames. His mind drifted far from the mountain to Lena's warm smile and the way Oliver and Audrey shouted 'Daddy!' as they raced to greet him after work. A wave of longing surged within him, a longing not just to be with them but to be *present* with them, something that had eluded him for far too long. How many moments had slipped by unnoticed, his mind tethered to work, stress and obligations, even while sitting at the dinner table? The ache of regret tightened in his chest, as heavy as the mountains surrounding him.

Eventually, he broke the silence, his voice fragile but honest. 'Sophia...' He hesitated for a moment. 'How do I find the *space within* when my mind never stops? It's always pushing – always thinking... analysing... planning. Sometimes I'm grateful for it. It's helped me achieve a lot. But at other times...' He sighed and looked into the flames. '...it feels like my greatest enemy. It prevents me for being present with those I love – and even with myself.'

Sophia's eyes softened, the firelight reflecting in them. 'It tells you things that hurt you, doesn't it?'

Andrew studied Sophia more closely. She wasn't merely speaking as some kind of oracle; her words seemed to hint at a shared experience. He nodded, his shoulders sagging under the weight of her observation. 'It tells me I'm not good enough. That I'll never be good enough. That I don't deserve what I have. And the worst part is…' He swallowed hard. 'Sometimes I believe it.'

Sophia let his words settle into the night, the crackling of the fire filling the space between them. Finally, she spoke, her voice calm and soothing. 'That's the nature of the mind. When left unchecked, it can become a powerful critic, planting doubts, fears and insecurities deep within us. And the problem isn't that the mind speaks to us – it always will. The problem is that you've been listening to it without questioning it.'

He leaned in, intrigued by her words. 'What exactly is happening in my mind?'

'Your mind has two main parts… the conscious and the subconscious. Your conscious mind is the one you're most aware of. It's deliberate. It makes plans, solves problems and acts. But your subconscious? It's quieter… deeper. It controls your emotions, your habits, even your beliefs. And every conscious thought you have – every doubt, every affirmation – is like a seed you're planting in your subconscious.'

Andrew frowned.

Sophia stood up, brushed the dirt from her hands and gestured for him to follow her. They walked to a patch of bare earth away from the fire where she knelt and drew a circle in the dirt with a stick.

'Imagine that within this circle lies your subconscious... It is soft, fertile soil, ready to receive any seed you plant.' She picked up a handful of small stones from the ground, spreading them between her hands. 'These stones represent the seeds – your conscious thoughts.

'Some...' She showed him some reddish-coloured stones in her left hand. '...are flower seeds... positive beliefs like *I am capable* or *I trust myself.*'

'Others are weed seeds.' She opened her left hand to reveal pale grey stones. 'Negative beliefs like *I'm not good enough* or *I'm going to fail.*'

Sophia dropped a few of the red stones into the dirt. 'When you plant these seeds, what will grow?'

'Flowers.' The metaphor began to take shape in Andrew's mind.

'And when you plant these seeds, what will grow?' she said, dropping the grey stones into the dirt.

'Weeds,' he said quietly.

'And here's the thing, Andrew... Your subconscious doesn't discriminate. It will grow whatever you plant. If you consistently plant negative thoughts, your mind will become overrun with weeds. They drain your energy, affecting your self-confidence. But when you plant positive thoughts, consciously nurturing positive beliefs, you grow flowers. Self-belief.

'And, over time, the state of your garden – the state of your subconscious – shapes the quality of your relationship with yourself and ultimately the quality of your life. Which is why it's very important to turn your subconscious into an ally instead of an enemy.'

THE TREE AND THE MOUNTAIN

Andrew stared at the circle, the metaphor sinking deeper with each passing moment. His mind flashed back to the doubts and self-criticism he had fed himself over the years. He could see it clearly now: his garden had become overgrown with weeds. 'How do I remove the weeds and start planting more flowers?' he asked, his tone expressing both desperation and hope.

Sophia smiled, her warmth filling the space between them. 'Every morning, plant a positive thought. Say to yourself, *I trust myself* or *I am enough*. Water that seed throughout the day by noticing your wins, no matter how small. The more you do, the more your garden will flourish. And remember, Andrew... you are the gardener. You have the power to choose what you plant.'

A newfound clarity filled Andrew's heart, like the first rays of dawn piercing through a dense fog. The path ahead wasn't about quieting his mind but nurturing it with intention. He envisioned each morning as an opportunity to plant seeds of positivity and purpose, allowing them to grow into something meaningful, something lasting. *Breakfast...* He'd start with breakfast. Time spent with Oliver and Audrey before they went to school – no more rushing out of the door. It would be a simple way to plant flowers each and every day.

Andrew remained kneeling in the dirt, letting his thoughts settle. Then, Sophia rose, her composure unwavering.

'It's time for me to go,' she said gently. 'You have everything you need to make it through the night. And tomorrow, you will climb. Godspeed.'

A wave of gratitude and bittersweet acceptance tightened Andrew's chest. He wanted to hold on to this moment, to the guidance she had given him, but he knew this was how it had to be. He nodded. 'Thank you, Sophia. For everything.'

She inclined her head, her expression serene. 'Thank *you*, Andrew. You've already paid me back in a way that you could not possibly know. Now, remember… let your heart guide, your mind execute and your energy speak. Together, they'll take you further than you've ever imagined.'

With that, she turned and disappeared into the shadows of the forest, the trees seeming to close behind her, leaving only the echo of her presence.

24

The Storm

The warmth of the fire lingered in Andrew's body as he stood up and stared at the dark expanse of forest behind him. It was time to turn in and get some rest before the trials of the morning. But his mind was buzzing with the insights Sophia had shared with him. He made a circuit of the encampment. Perhaps it would be better if he spent just a few minutes determining his direction for the morning trek. His boots crunched softly on the forest floor as he moved away from the lake and into the darkness. Above him, the branches whispered in the cool night air, a murmur that seemed to grow louder the further he walked.

The forest thickened, the shadows deepening. The air turned colder, sharper, as if the night itself had secrets it was waiting to reveal. Just as he began to wonder if he should turn back, a silvery mist appeared, snaking its way around his boots like the tendrils of an unseen force. At first, it was delicate, harmless, even beautiful. But within moments, it thickened, rising up his legs and enveloping his midriff in a dense haze.

He spun around. In the distance the faint, amber light of the fire flickered. His heart raced and panic clawed at his chest. He quickened his pace but the mist clung to him, brushing his skin like cold, unwelcome hands.

Then the rain began. It fell softly at first, then harder, before drenching him in sheets of icy water. The forest floor turned slick and muddy beneath his boots, while the mist pressed closer, suffocating him in its cold grip.

'Stay calm,' he muttered, but the words were hollow amid the emerging chaos.

His boot caught in a root and he stumbled, crashing to the ground. The impact jarred his body, and cold mud seeped into his clothes, clinging to him like the heavy mantle of everything he had carried for years. Rain lashed at his back as he lay motionless, voices within him rising like a tidal wave.

Loser! You've failed. Sophia has only just left and you're already lost. You'll never make it. This is who you are... lost, broken, unworthy.

The words tore at him, dragging him deeper into the mud, into despair. He clenched his fists, squeezing handfuls of wet earth as if trying to ground himself, but the voices only grew louder, the volume unbearable.

Those damn weeds!

He pushed himself to his knees, spitting out dirt, his breath coming in ragged gasps. Above him the storm raged on, the rain hammering down, the mud sucking him down. His surroundings blurred. There was nothing but the mist, the darkness and the relentless cacophony inside his head.

'Help!' he shouted into the storm, his voice cracking. 'Somebody help me!'

The thundering rain drowned out his cries. Fear, cold and merciless, gripped him, whispering that he would vanish into the night and be forgotten. Memories surfaced... moments of childhood pain... of being bullied, ignored, rejected... abandoned. The wounds he had buried deep gaped wide open.

Desperation tightened around him like a noose. He squeezed his eyes shut and clutched his chest, forcing himself to breathe – the one thing he could control. *In... out. In... out.* Slowly, the pounding of his heart eased, while the storm raged around him.

Then a voice broke through the storm. At first, he thought he was imagining it, but then it came again, soft but insistent, cutting through the roar of the rain.

'Stand up.'

Andrew's eyes flew open and there, before him, was a boy with dark, damp hair and piercing blue eyes that glowed like beacons. He extended a hand.

'Come with me.' The boy's voice was calm.

Andrew hesitated, but the boy's gaze held him, grounding him in spite of the storm raging around him. Slowly, Andrew reached out and grasped the boy's hand. It was warm, firm... real. With surprising strength, the boy pulled him to his feet.

'Where are we going?' Andrew asked, his voice hoarse.

'To safety,' the boy said simply, turning and leading him away.

Andrew followed, his steps unsteady but driven by the boy's unwavering confidence. The rain pelted them and the mud clung to his boots, but the boy moved through the forest as if he knew it by heart. The mist parted before him, and Andrew clung to the hope that this strange child could guide him out of the chaos.

They weaved through the trees, their surroundings blurring until Andrew saw the towering silhouette of a rock face rising above them. The boy stopped at its base and pointed to a narrow opening.

'Here,' he said. Without hesitation, he slipped inside.

Andrew followed, squeezing through the gap into a dry, sheltered cave. The sound of the rain faded and the air inside was cool and still. Andrew collapsed onto a flat stone, his body trembling from cold and exhaustion.

Moving swiftly, the boy collected wood from a small pile stacked neatly in a corner. Within moments, he had lit a fire, the flames casting a warm, golden glow that filled the cave. The warmth seeped into Andrew's bones as he wrapped himself in the woven blanket the boy handed him.

'Thank you for saving me,' Andrew said, his voice still shaky.

The boy smiled, but there was something unusual in his eyes – something ancient, as though he carried wisdom far beyond his years. He couldn't have been much older than Oliver. He wasn't unlike Oliver, in fact, though lacking the dimples he and Audrey shared with Lena.

Renewed thoughts of Lena, Oliver and Audrey cut into Andrew like a dagger. He leaned closer to the fire. 'Who are you? And what are you doing here?'

The boy looked at him calmly, his expression serene. 'I am Shuka. I've been waiting for you.'

25

Self-Belief

Sitting cross-legged, his damp clothes clinging to him, Andrew calmed his breathing as the tension in his chest slowly unwound.

Across from him, Shuka was sitting quietly, his small frame bathed in the golden light of the flames. He observed Andrew with a patient understanding, as though waiting for him to let down the last wall. There was something comforting about Shuka, as if he carried the weight of centuries but was still light enough to laugh.

Andrew cleared his throat, his words emerging cautiously. 'You said you've been waiting for me. How? Why?'

Shuka leaned forwards slightly, studying Andrew with a piercing look that seemed to see past the soaked clothes and exhausted exterior. 'Out in the storm you were afraid, right? Truly afraid.' His voice was as constant as the fire's crackle.

Andrew shivered, reliving the fear of being lost, trapped in the storm with no way out.

Shuka smiled. 'I heard your call. Help comes to those who seek it.'

'You heard my call?'

Shuka nodded. 'Fear signals to those who understand it.' He shifted slightly, resting his elbows on his knees.

'I've known fear all my life. But I know now that there are two kinds... fear that holds you back and fear that drives you forwards.'

Andrew leaned in, his eyes widening. Something about the boy's words struck a chord within him. 'What do you mean?'

'There are the fears that paralyse me,' Shuka explained, staring into the flames. 'The fear of failing... the fear of being judged... the fear of the unknown... Those particular fears keep me frozen, trapped inside my mind. But then there are other fears, the fears that drive me... for instance, the fear of wasting my potential... of never being seen... of being alone forever. Those drive me to act... to connect... to be better.'

Andrew frowned. He knew those fears well. His life had been shaped by that same tension, the constant push and pull between not feeling sufficient and desperately trying to prove he was. 'I've felt that too,' he murmured. 'I've built my entire life around trying to avoid failure.'

Shuka tilted his head, curiosity flickering across his face. 'And has it worked?'

Andrew sighed, the significance of the question settling upon him. 'It's made me successful. At least, by most people's standards. But I'm not sure if it's made me happy.'

Shuka's gaze softened. 'Fear can be a powerful compass. But it often points us in the wrong direction.'

Andrew swallowed hard. 'And yet, I don't know if I've ever lived without it. I don't know what would happen if I didn't allow myself to be driven by it.'

'There's something else that can drive you,' Shuka said. 'Yourself.'

Andrew blinked, confused. 'But I'm already guiding myself, aren't I?'

'No.' Shuka smiled faintly. 'Right now, fear is guiding you. You're not listening to who you really are. You're listening to what you're afraid of.'

'And how do I change that?'

Shuka stood up and tossed a log onto the fire. Sparks shot upwards, lighting up the cave in a burst of warmth and life. 'Look at the walls around you.'

Andrew turned away from the fire. Primitive drawings of animals and stick figures covered the stone around them – raw... expressive... alive. In the flickering glow of the firelight, they appeared to be locked in an ancient battle for survival, their shadows jousting and twisting, the cave pulsing with a strange energy. Andrew felt a peculiar shift deep within him, as if he'd been joined by the presence of many. The cave had transformed into something more... a bridge to a distant past, to where it all began. And, slowly, the message began to dawn on him.

'I come here to imagine their stories,' Shuka said, wistfully. 'The epic journeys they took... their heroic battles with wild animals... the great distances they walked in search of food and shelter. I see them enduring the bitter winters. But, most of all, I come to listen – to connect with them through space and time.' Shuka glanced at Andrew, as if searching for recognition.

Andrew gave Shuka a warm smile, confirming that he was beginning to understand. He traced the dancing shadows with his eyes; their movements were hypnotic.

THE TREE AND THE MOUNTAIN

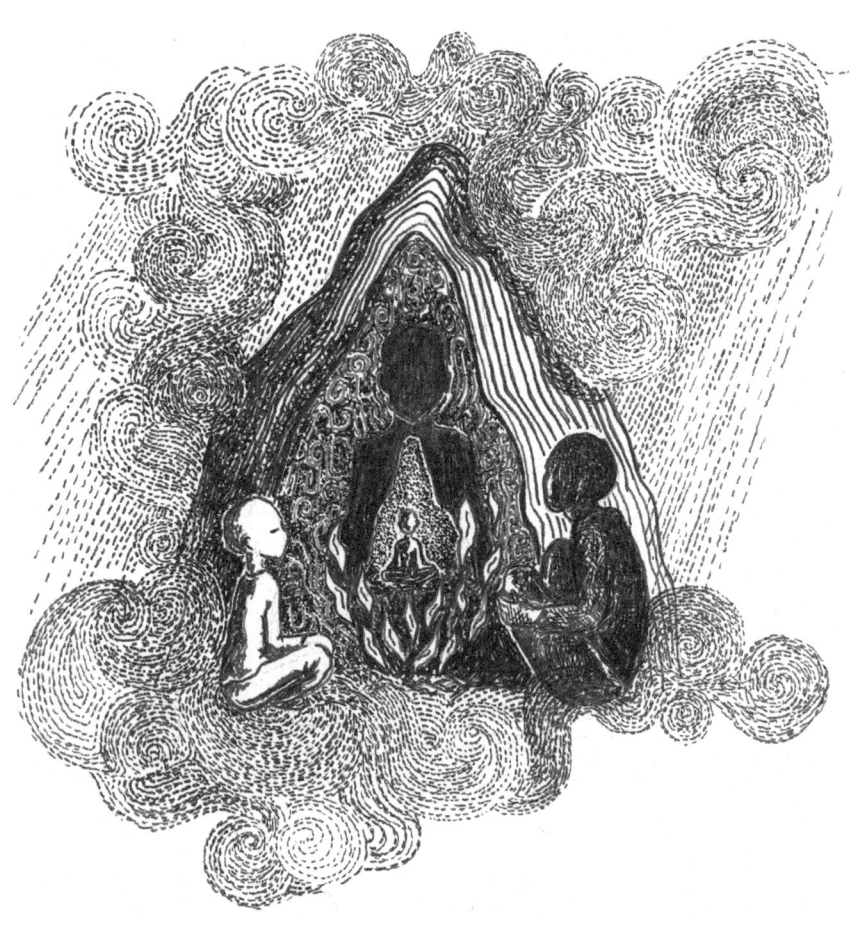

'It's here within these walls,' Shuka said, 'that I begin to know what it truly means to be me.'

Andrew leaned forwards. 'What do you mean?'

'I can feel the energy of all those who came before me – the women and men whose choices, struggles and resilience shaped me. When I imagine their lives, I sense the full spectrum of what it means to be human... love and betrayal... joy and sorrow... fear and forgiveness... anger and grace. It's all there, echoing through time.' Shuka fell silent for a moment, letting the fire crackle between them. 'The drawings are here because the people who made them believed their lives mattered. They lived with purpose. But they also knew their time was brief, and that what they left behind wouldn't just be marks on stone. It would be the essence of who they were.'

A thought struck Andrew: had even one moment in his ancestors' lives unfolded differently, he wouldn't be here. Certainly not in this form, in this place, sitting with Shuka in a mountain cave while a storm raged outside. 'Had our parents made different choices,' he said, 'had our grandparents taken a different path... we might never have existed. And yet... here we are.'

Shuka's voice became almost a whisper. 'Theirs are the voices you need to listen to... not the fear, not the doubts. You need to listen to who you are beneath all that.'

Andrew's heart pounded in his chest, his breathing quickening. 'But I don't know how. All I hear is noise... the doubts... the fears.'

THE TREE AND THE MOUNTAIN

Shuka placed a hand on Andrew's shoulder, grounding him. 'It starts with silence. Not outside, but inside. You have to be willing to sit with the noise until it disappears.'

Heeding the invitation, Andrew closed his eyes, focusing on his breathing as the storm outside faded into the background. The fire crackled softly, familiar and comforting. But his mind still raced, clinging to fears he had carried for years. For what felt like an eternity, he struggled to find inner calm.

Shuka's voice cut through his internal chaos. 'You're not alone in this, Andrew. Your ancestors... they faced the same struggles. They left behind their strength, their resilience, so you wouldn't have to carry everything on your own. Feel their presence. Listen to their story.'

Opening his eyes, Andrew looked up at the stick figures as they danced in the flickering light. He saw their struggles and triumphs, their resilience and determination to survive. He was the latest link in a chain stretching back through time, each generation adding its own chapter to a shared story. Their sacrifices, their hopes, their victories... he carried all of it within him.

And then, as if summoned by the flickering fire, scenes from Andrew's own life appeared before him: the forced smiles... the missed family dinners... the late nights hunched over his work. The folly of his choices pressed down on him and a wave of unworthiness washed over him. Had he let his ancestors down? Had he squandered the opportunities they had fought so hard to give him?

Tears blurred his vision. 'I feel like I've failed them.'

Shuka leaned forwards, laying a comforting hand on Andrew's knee. 'Do you think they never doubted themselves? Do you think they didn't feel fear or wonder if they were enough?'

Andrew looked again at the figures on the wall that were standing tall and confident, some holding spears as if preparing for battle. 'Maybe they did. But they didn't show it.'

Shuka smiled faintly. 'Exactly. They weren't perfect. They knew it. But they believed in their ability to move forward. And that belief carried them through.'

Andrew's breath hitched as the truth settled into him like a seed planted in fertile soil. He had been projecting confidence outwardly but, inside, he had been lost. He had sought validation through his achievements but it had never been enough. Self-belief, he realised, couldn't come from external success. It had to grow from within.

'Do you believe in yourself?' Shuka's voice was gentle but direct.

Andrew hesitated. His mind wanted to say yes but his heart whispered the truth. 'No,' he admitted. 'Not really.'

'Then maybe,' Shuka said softly, 'it's time to stop trying to earn your worth through achievements. Maybe it's time to meet the most important person you'll ever know and build a better relationship with them.'

Andrew looked up, his mind swirling in confusion. 'Who's that?'

Shuka's eyes sparkled with warmth. 'It's *you*.'

26

Inner Confidence

Shuka tossed more branches onto the fire, watching as the flames flared and settled. He continued to stare into the embers for a moment before turning back to Andrew, his eyes reflective, thoughtful. 'So many of us build our confidence from the outside in. We rely on achievements to feel strong, as if we're borrowing that strength and hoping it'll sink in over time.'

Andrew nodded, feeling the truth of it in his bones. 'Borrowing confidence,' he murmured. 'That's exactly what it feels like. But you think there's another way?'

Shuka smiled faintly, his warmth mirroring that of the fire. 'What if, instead of borrowing it, you built it directly from the source?'

Andrew tilted his head to one side. 'The source?'

'Let me show you.' Shuka raised a clenched fist, holding it firmly between them. 'Imagine this is you. On the outside, it looks solid and strong. This is what we show the world, right?' He invited Andrew to touch it.

Andrew pressed his hand against Shuka's fist. It was firm and unyielding.

'This is what others see,' Shuka said. 'Confidence. Assurance. Strength.'

Slowly, Shuka unfurled his fingers, revealing the soft palm within. 'But inside it's different, isn't it?'

Andrew touched Shuka's open palm. It was soft, vulnerable. The opposite of the strength he had felt moments before.

'Inside here,' Shuka said quietly, 'is where our confidence lies. The place of doubts… of wondering if we're enough… of fearing others will see us as we secretly see ourselves. We tend to hide this part to protect ourselves.'

Andrew's throat tightened. His public image had always been one of confidence, of leadership. Yet privately he often questioned why anyone believed it. 'So how do we close the gap between what we project and what we feel?'

Shuka smiled. 'By understanding the dynamics of confidence, and by taking action.'

Andrew nodded and grinned.

Shuka clenched his fist again, tracing circles around it with his finger. 'We build layers around ourselves, circles of connection… our family… our friends… even strangers. We rely on their opinions to tell us who we are, to feel worthy, to feel enough. But that's where the problem begins. When we allow others to become our primary reference point, we hand them the power to define our self-worth.'

Andrew's breath caught, realisation settling over him like a heavy blanket.

'We chase achievements for the same reason,' Shuka continued. 'We hope that if we accomplish enough, people will see us as valuable and that, somehow, we'll believe it too. But that's not where our worth comes from.' He opened his hand again and pressed it firmly against his chest. 'Our true worth is here. Inside. Not out there.'

Andrew exhaled sharply, as if releasing years of unspoken tension. 'So, it's like...' He searched for the right words. 'It's like waiting for the people around us to give us their permission to see ourselves differently when, in fact, we have never needed it.'

Shuka's eyes lit up. 'That's right! Real confidence begins when you stop looking outwards for validation and instead look in the mirror.'

Andrew stared at his hands as if seeing them with new eyes. 'So, I need to stop letting others define me?'

'Yes.'

'How?'

'Learn to give yourself what you've been searching for from others. Start from the inside and let it flow outwards.'

Andrew let the idea sink in, a quiet calm spreading through him. 'So, instead of waiting for others to respect me, I need to learn how to respect myself first?'

'Yes. And the irony is this:

'By respecting yourself – setting boundaries, valuing your time – you'll naturally earn the respect of others who admire that strength.

'By trusting your intuition, you'll dare to speak up and lead, gaining the trust of those who seek guidance.

'By believing in yourself, acting in alignment with your values, you'll inspire others, not because you're trying to, but because they'll see the strength of your character.

'It all begins with how you treat yourself. The courage to be *you*.'

Andrew felt something click, another puzzle piece sliding into place. For so long, he had chased external achievements to fill an internal void. But here was the missing piece, a way to be whole without needing the validation of the outside world.

He thought of the journey that had brought him here – descending from the top of the tree, reaching the base of the mountain, beginning the climb and now sitting in this cave, illuminated by the firelight. Every step, every encounter, every lesson had been guiding him towards this moment, teaching him how to trust, believe in and maybe even love himself.

'The key,' he said boldly, 'is to stop chasing outside what I need to cultivate inside.'

Shuka smiled as if he had been waiting for Andrew to reach that conclusion. 'Yes. And it takes courage. Courage to face yourself. Courage to prevent fear from taking the lead. Courage to trust that who you are is already enough.'

Andrew nodded, the truth of Shuka's words resonating deeply. He had shown courage in many external situations throughout his life, but had he ever truly turned that courage inwards? Had he ever directed it towards embracing his authentic self? The answer was clear: he hadn't. But that could change now.

'You've given me something powerful,' Andrew said quietly, his voice thick with gratitude.

Shuka shook his head gently. 'It was always there. Sometimes, we just need to get lost in a storm to find what's missing.'

Andrew smiled. 'And I think you may be the bravest person I've ever met.'

Shuka lowered his head. 'May I make one request of you?'

'Of course!'

'Please don't forget me.'

For the first time since meeting him, Andrew saw the vulnerability of a child in the boy.

'I'll never forget you, Shuka. I swear.'

Shuka wrapped his arms around Andrew in a warm embrace, the connection grounding them both. It wasn't just comfort; it was a moment of recognition, of understanding.

When they finally drew back, they both turned towards the cave's entrance. The storm had passed, leaving behind a serene, moonlit night. The air smelled fresh, cleansed by the rain. They laughed, realising how completely they had lost track of time.

Andrew looked out into the darkness and the unfamiliar forest. 'Where do I go from here?' he asked Shuka.

'The surest way is back to your encampment,' said Shuka, pointing to the path that led back to the lake. 'There, be sure to get some sleep in your shelter. Once the sun rises, the rest of the journey will be yours to complete.'

Andrew felt weary but confident. With a final wave, he stepped out into the night, the crisp air filling his lungs. He no longer felt the strain of the journey. He felt its purpose. And the courage to continue.

THE TREE AND THE MOUNTAIN

27

Deep Fear

A ndrew moved silently through the forest, each step drawing him deeper into the shadowy woods. The storm had left the air cool and still, rich with the scent of damp earth and pine needles. The freshness of the earth seemed to echo the shift he felt within himself: a profound clarity, as though he had stepped into a new version of himself. Each step felt purposeful, yet with every stride into the dark woods, a creeping unease began to stir.

The canopy above blotted out most of the starlight, leaving only faint silver threads weaving through the branches. The air grew heavier, the earlier calm replaced by an intangible dread slithering into Andrew's mind like a predator stalking its prey. He stopped abruptly, straining to hear any sound beyond the crunch of his own footsteps and the steady rhythm of his breathing. The silence was deafening, bearing down on him like the bulk of the mountain itself.

Suddenly, a sharp crack split the air to his right, echoing through the trees like a gunshot. Andrew froze, his heart hammering in his chest. He turned sharply towards the noise, but the darkness held only shadows that shifted and blended into one another. 'It's nothing,' he muttered to himself, his voice a fragile thread of reassurance. But even as the words left his lips, a low, guttural growl reached his ears, sending chills rippling down his spine.

From the shadows, a pair of glowing eyes appeared. Amber orbs, flickering like embers in the darkness. Another pair blinked into view. And another. Andrew held his breath as the glowing eyes multiplied, surrounding him. Wolves. An entire pack. Their silhouettes emerged from the gloom, their movements slow and deliberate. From the centre of the pack, the leader stepped forwards – a massive creature with a black coat that gleamed in the faint starlight. Its eyes burned with a piercing, ancient intelligence and its growl rumbled through the forest like distant thunder.

Fear, icy and unrelenting, gripped Andrew, rooting him to the spot. His mind screamed at him to run, but his legs wouldn't move. He took a single step backwards, then another, but the wolves closed in, their glowing eyes reflecting his terror. Their movements were coordinated, predatory; they were feeding off his fear. The leader lowered its head slightly, its piercing gaze fixed on Andrew, as though reading his every thought.

From the depths of his mind, a voice slithered forth. *What did you expect?* it sneered, sharp and mocking. It was the voice of one of his inner critics, the relentless goblins who had always showed up in his darkest moments. Another voice joined in, shrill and venomous. *You thought you were strong, but look at you now. Weak. Helpless!*

Andrew's breath quickened, panic blooming in his chest. The voices multiplied, swirling in his mind like a hurricane, each one cutting deeper than the last. *You've always been a*

DEEP FEAR

failure, one hissed. *You'll never be good enough.* Their taunts grew louder, more vicious, drowning out even the growls of the wolves.

The pack continued to advance slowly, their growls harmonising with the storm in his mind. Catching a foot on a root, he fell onto his backside, his arms sticking into the cold, wet earth. Mud covered his hands and trousers, the weight of fear crushing him. The voices tore at him, clawing at his self-worth, threatening to destroy him.

And then, through the chaos, memories flickered: Santi's calm strength. Sophia's grounding wisdom. Shuka's infectious courage. Each of them had shared something with him, igniting sparks of resilience within. Slowly, those sparks began to grow, pushing back against the suffocating darkness in his mind.

Andrew thought of his Power of Nine – his values, his talents, his aspirations. They anchored him, lifted him and guided him. He saw the faces of his wife and children, their love radiant and unwavering, cutting through the icy grip of despair. He remembered his ancestors, their stories etched into the cave walls, their presence an unbroken thread connecting him to the strength of generations past.

His breathing slowed. The storm within him began to calm. Slowly, he pushed himself to his knees, his hands trembling. The taunts in his head faltered, losing their power. Looking upwards, he locked eyes with the wolf leader. The creature's amber eyes blazed with challenge, but there was something else there too… curiosity.

'I am not afraid of you,' Andrew said, his voice low but firm. The words were spoken quietly, but they carried a magnitude that filled the forest. The wolves paused, their circling slowing. The leader tilted its head slightly, as if considering him.

Andrew rose to his feet, his movements slow and controlled. 'I am strong and free,' he said, his voice a little louder. He took a step forwards. 'I have my place in this world.'

Another step. The wolves hesitated, their glowing eyes flickering like candles in the wind.

'I trust myself,' Andrew declared, his voice growing stronger with each word, with each step.

The leader stood firm, unmoving.

'I believe in me!' Andrew shouted, his voice ringing out like a battle cry. The words echoed through the forest, carried on the wind.

The wolf leader was within striking distance, a shadow of power and intent. Its golden eyes burned into Andrew's, unwavering, unyielding. The air between them crackled with tension, every muscle in the wolf's body poised for the inevitable.

But Andrew did not flinch. Standing tall, he chose to face this moment head-on – not as a man cowering in fear but as the truest version of himself. Images surged in his mind... his ancestors with their raised spears, their faces fierce and resolute, their belief in their purpose unshakeable. He saw the figures etched on the cave walls, symbols of resilience and courage passed down through time. In that moment, he understood: *I am them, and they are me.*

His willpower became his spear, his belief his shield. The strength that had carried his ancestors through their own battles coursed through him. He met the wolf leader's piercing eyes and smiled – not a smile of defiance or bravado but one of peace. It was a smile that acknowledged both life and death, the twin forces that danced within every moment of existence. For the first time, Andrew saw them as one, inseparable and essential. A single tear escaped down his cheek as a deep, steadfast calm settled over him.

The wolf leader lowered its head slowly, its long, narrow chin brushing the earth. Its body shifted, muscles taut, preparing for the strike.

Andrew knew the moment had arrived, that razor-thin edge where everything would be decided. He stood his ground, his breathing stable, his heart beating calmly. He was ready to accept his fate, whatever that may be.

The wolf leader closed its eyes unexpectedly, its powerful frame softening. It remained still, its mighty presence now free of aggression, as if the tension had been replaced with something ancient and sacred.

Andrew felt a pull from within, a wordless invitation to bridge the gap between them. Trusting the instinct rising in his chest, he stepped forwards cautiously. The pack watched him, their glowing eyes unblinking, their forms frozen in anticipation. Even the forest seemed to hold its breath, as though nature itself awaited what would happen next.

When he reached the wolf leader, he knelt slowly, keeping his movements deliberate, reverent. Extending his hand, he placed it gently on the creature's forehead. The fur was coarse and rough, its warmth pulsing beneath his palm. Andrew closed his eyes, inhaling deeply.

Time dissolved, the boundaries between man and beast, fear and courage, dissolving with it. In that silence, a bond formed – raw and primal yet profoundly tender. He felt the wolf's strength, its instinct, its wisdom and, in return, he offered his own. He felt the presence of his ancestors surround him, their spirits standing as witnesses to this moment. The forest whispered its approval. Two forces once poised for battle now aligned in mutual respect, the barriers between them replaced by a shared truth.

For the first time, Andrew felt a complete absence of fear. Not just the absence of immediate terror but of the deeper, more insidious fears that had haunted him for years. In their place was a quiet, immutable truth: he *belonged* – to himself, to the world, to the greater tapestry of existence.

The pack leader opened its eyes, holding Andrew's gaze for a heartbeat longer before turning and melting back into the shadows. One by one, the pack followed, their glowing eyes fading into the darkness, leaving Andrew alone beneath the canopy of stars.

Andrew remained kneeling for a moment, his breathing coming in slow, deliberate waves. His heart started pounding with the realisation of what had just transpired, yet his soul felt lighter than it had in years. As he rose to his feet, his legs buckled, and he sank back to the ground, his body overcome with emotion.

Lying motionless on the forest floor, he let the tears come. They flowed freely, carrying with them years of fear, self-doubt and the relentless voices that had haunted him. With each tear, he felt the burden lifting, the chains loosening.

Above him, the stars gleamed brighter than ever, as if the universe itself was acknowledging his transformation. And in the silence of the forest, a profound peace settled over him. He was free.

After recovering his strength, he resumed his journey back to the lake and the encampment. Upon arrival, he nestled inside the shelter. Releasing a long sigh, he shed the last vestiges of his old self and fell asleep.

28

The Climb

Andrew stirred as the soft morning light filtered through the forest canopy into his shelter. A symphony of birdsong rang out, signalling a new day. There was something irresistible about nature's awakening. No matter how fatigued or frustrated one might be, each sunrise carried the promise of something new, a fresh start, a new opportunity. Today felt particularly special; the summit was within reach.

He stretched, the cool air filling his lungs as he stepped outside. The forest around him pulsed with energy. As he inhaled deeply, his thoughts settled on the lessons of his journey so far: the wisdom of Santi, Sophia and Shuka; the clarity he had gained; the fear he had faced and overcome. He felt a strength within himself he hadn't known existed.

Standing tall, he grounded himself in his Power of Nine. He imagined his ship, its hull strong with his values, its sails filled by his talents and its course guided by his aspirations. 'Today,' he whispered to himself, 'I will be the best version of me.' The words settled into his core like a promise. He had planted his first seed of the day: a flower seed.

As he left the lakeside shelter, he looked up at the mountain that loomed ahead. Today was the day he would reach the summit, the goal that had driven him since he had begun his journey – his portal home. With every step, the forest thinned, its lush greenery giving way to the raw, exposed rock of the mountain's upper reaches.

The incline steepened gradually at first, challenging but manageable. The air grew thinner and the wind sharpened, cutting through his clothes as if testing his resolve. The terrain became harsher, the path littered with loose scree and jagged stones that shifted underfoot. Andrew focused on each step, breathing calmly, his mind locked on the summit.

By mid-afternoon, the path had disappeared entirely, replaced by a vertical wall of rock that loomed above him, its pointed edges clawing at the sky. It wasn't just an obstacle – it felt like a final challenge, a gatekeeper barring his way to the summit. The sheer height of it made his stomach churn and he hesitated, his eyes flicking between the unyielding wall and the endless drop below.

Was this the mountain's final test?

Andrew stepped forwards, placing a tentative hand on the cold stone. The rough surface bit into his palm, grounding him in the reality of the climb. His heart pounded as he scanned the rock face, searching for handholds and footholds. There was no way around it. He would have to climb.

'You've faced worse,' he muttered, more to himself than to the mountain. But even as he said it, a flicker of doubt crept in. What if he couldn't do it? What if he fell?

Shaking his head, he pushed the thoughts aside. He tightened his grip on the rock, testing its stability, and began to climb.

THE CLIMB

The ascent was brutal. Each movement required every ounce of his strength and focus. His muscles screamed in protest and his fingers were raw from gripping the unforgiving stone. The higher he climbed, the fiercer the wind howled, battering him from every angle. Rocks shifted beneath his feet, threatening to send him tumbling. His breath came in sharp bursts, his vision narrowing to the next hold, the next ledge. His world condensed into a rhythm: grip, pull, step, breathe.

Midway up, he paused on a narrow outcrop, his legs dangling over the dizzying drop below. He glanced down at the valley, now a blur of green and shadow far below, and a wave of vertigo swept over him. For a moment his confidence wavered. Memories of his life flashed before him – the relentless chase for success, the moments of doubt, the constant striving to prove himself.

Why am I really here? The question burned in his mind. *Am I climbing to prove something or to find something?*

He forced himself to keep moving, his focus sharpening as he neared the top of the wall. But just as he reached for the next handhold, the rock beneath his foot crumbled. His balance wavered and his heart leapt into his throat.

For a split second, he hung from his fingers, his grip slipping, his body trembling. Panic surged through him like a tidal wave. His breath caught, and the familiar voices of doubt roared into life. *You can't do this. You're not strong enough.*

Tears stung his eyes as he clung to the rock, his fingers aching, his strength fading. The wind howled, mocking him, as if the mountain itself were taunting him for his failure. He closed his eyes, the storm of doubt threatening to overwhelm him.

It happened in an instant.

He let go.

As he fell through the air, a feeling of despair swept through him. The fall seemed like an eternity, his body hitting a hard ledge below. He lay on his back immobile, unable to move or breathe, before everything turned to black.

29

The Chance

Andrew's descent into the blackness was absolute. A consuming void had swallowed him whole, and he felt as though he were falling endlessly, spinning into an abyss without form, without light, without end. There was no mountain any more, no summit, no wolves – just an infinite, suffocating nothingness.

But then, faintly, as if from the furthest edges of his awareness, came a sound. Continuous and rhythmic.

Beep. Beep. Beep.

It pierced the blackness, each tone a lifeline reaching out to him. Andrew tried to grab hold of it and pull himself towards the sound, but his senses were sluggish, disjointed. Awareness struggled to return, fractured and incomplete. The sound grew louder, sharper, dragging him upwards through the heavy fog that bound him.

Gradually, other sensations emerged – a heaviness weighing down his body, as if he was encased in lead; a chill creeping through his limbs; the rough press of something firm beneath him. He tried to move, but his muscles betrayed him. He was immobile, trapped within himself. Panic surged like a jolt of electricity and he fought against the restraints of his body, willing his arms to move, his eyes to open, but nothing responded.

The beeping persisted, relentless and unyielding, a cruel metronome ticking away the seconds of his helplessness.

Then came the voices.

First came distant murmurs, soft and indistinct, but they soon sharpened. Familiar words broke through, and with them, the unmistakable voice of Lena, his wife.

'Is there anything more we can do, Doctor? Anything at all?' Her words were strained, each syllable heavy with desperation. He could feel her pain, even through the suffocating fog that was enveloping him.

A second voice followed, calm and clinical. 'I'm afraid we've done all we can. The injuries were severe. Significant trauma to the spine and head. We've stabilised him for now, but he has to do the rest. It's up to him whether he fights. Whether he... pulls through.'

Andrew's heart twisted, though he couldn't feel it beating. The words *fights* and *pulls through* reverberated in his mind, their meaning cutting through the haze. He wasn't just hurt – he was on the edge, teetering between life and death.

He heard Lena again, her voice trembling. 'But... is he in pain? Can he... can he hear us, Doctor?'

The doctor hesitated. 'It's difficult to say. Some studies suggest patients in his condition may have moments of awareness. But there's no way to know for sure.'

Andrew wanted to scream, *Yes! I'm here! I can hear you!* But his body remained silent, locked in this twilight state. Despair welled within him, an agonising helplessness unlike anything he'd ever felt, and Lena's pain pressed heavily on him, heavier than the mountain.

'I don't want to lose him,' she whispered.

Lena's words cracked something within him. He thought of her standing beside his motionless body, fighting for him even when he couldn't fight for himself. He thought of his children... bright smiles... laughing eyes... tiny hands reaching for him when he walked through the door. He thought of everything he had yet to say to them, everything he still had to do – to *be*.

I'm not ready to leave, he thought fiercely. *I can't.*

As if responding to the fire that had sparked within him, the fog shifted, thinning ever so slightly. The beeping grew sharper, closer. He clung to it, using it as a lifeline, his mind resisting the darkness that was trying to pull him back under.

And then, just as the light seemed within reach, the doctor's words rang out again, quieter this time. 'If he doesn't show any improvement soon... it may be time to prepare for the worst.'

The world cracked. Lena's quiet 'I understand' sliced through him like a blade.

No. No, I won't let go.

And then, as if by a cruel twist of fate, the darkness folded in, consuming the last shreds of his awareness.

THE TREE AND THE MOUNTAIN

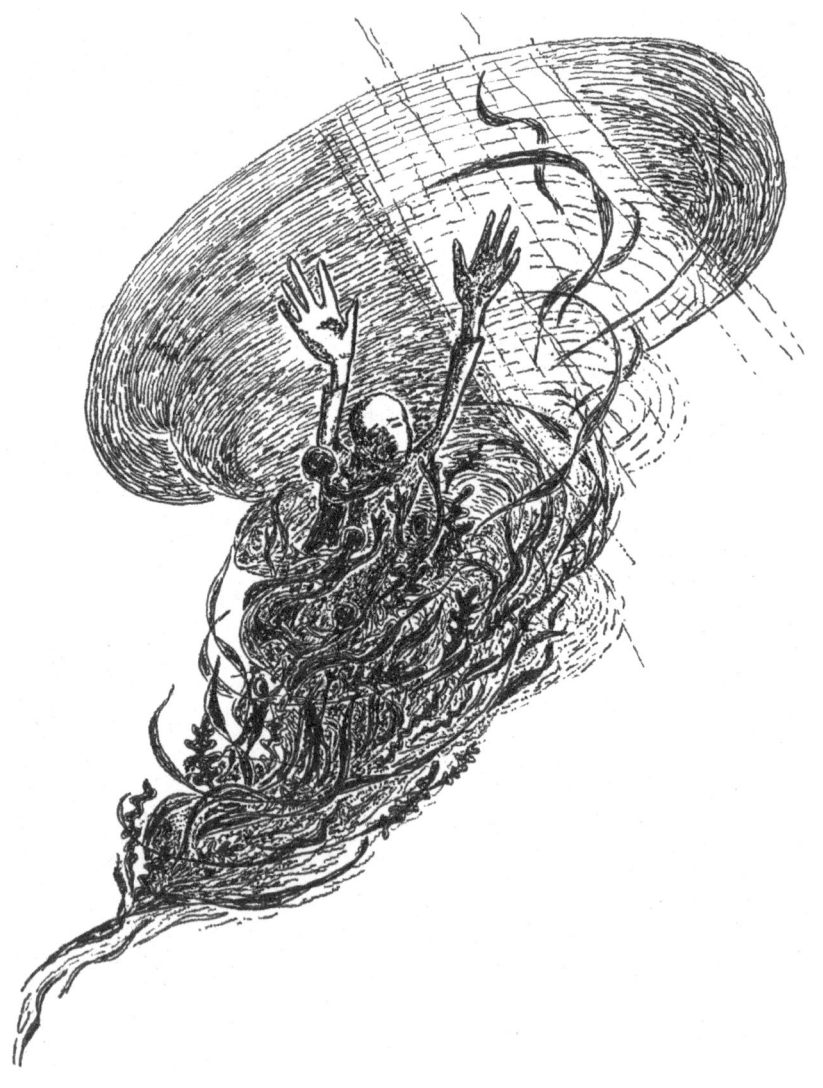

30

The Ledge

The beeping had faded, replaced by the roar of the wind, but the pain remained. As Andrew stirred on a jagged ledge, every inch of his body throbbed in agony, as if the mountain itself had carved its mark into his flesh. His ribs ached with every breath, his fingers throbbing and torn, but it was the ache in his chest that hurt the most – the same hollow, relentless pain he had felt in the hospital room. Between life and death. The same choice looming over him.

He sat up slowly, his breath ragged. He tried to corral his thoughts but Lena's voice echoed in his mind. *I don't want to lose him.* The sadness in her voice had nearly destroyed him. *It's up to him whether he fights.*

He pressed his hand against the freezing rock, trying to ground himself. The mountain wasn't a dream. It wasn't a symbol. It was here. The stakes were high. If he didn't reach the summit, he knew with chilling certainty that he would die – on this mountain and in that hospital bed.

Summoning every ounce of strength, Andrew forced himself to his feet, his legs trembling with exhaustion. Above him loomed the rock face that had spat him out, a wall that seemed intent on swallowing him whole again. Just out of sight, beyond the ledge, the summit waited. He was sure of it.

His breath came in shallow gasps as he found his first handhold – and hauled himself up. His muscles screamed with every pull, every desperate reach for a higher hold. His fingers, numb and bloodied, slipped more than once, but each time he clung tighter, refusing to let go. He couldn't afford to fall. Not here. Not now. Not again.

As he climbed, memories of Santi's calm wisdom and Sophia's unwavering belief in him surfaced again. Shuka's fearless courage echoed through his mind like a battle cry. With each reminder, he pulled himself higher, finding new reserves of strength hidden beneath the fatigue.

But it wasn't enough to just climb. The mental war raged as fiercely as the mountain's brutal winds. His mind was a battlefield of doubt, begging him to give up, to rest, to surrender. But his children's faces pierced through the noise. Their laughter. Their future. His heart ached for them, an ache far stronger than his pain.

But the pain was overpowering, unrelenting, and he was conscious of his energy draining away. And then came a voice, still clear and calm... *It's all right, Andrew... it's all right...* And then came another, as comforting as a summer breeze... *You've done so well, Andrew. Magnificently well. Better than anybody could have done. Now it's finished and you can rest.* The voices eased his anguish like balm. *It's enough. You've done your best – and nobody can ask for more than that... Lena and the children will miss you, of course, but they'll be fine... They'll have good lives and they'll remember you fondly... how brave you were and how much you loved them... But now it's time to rest... to let go... as eventually we all must...*

'Wait!' snarled Andrew. 'I know you!' These were the same voices that so often told him he was doomed to fail, that things couldn't be done – not by him. The sneers had gone but the message was the same – just wrapped differently and all the more vile for its insidious duplicity.

Andrew's scream tore from his guts in visceral defiance. '*No!*'

He would fight, whatever the outcome. This is what pulling through felt like. Pushing forwards when your body screamed no, when your mind was consumed with doubt, when every part of you begged for relief. He had to keep moving.

With one final push, fuelled by desperation and love, he gripped the edge of the final ledge. His body trembled violently, his hands barely able to hold on. But he knew this was it – the moment that would decide everything.

'Come on!' he snarled through gritted teeth, his voice barely audible over the howling wind. 'I believe in me!' he yelled.

With a final desperate effort, he summoned every ounce of strength left in his battered body. His muscles quivered, screaming for mercy as he gripped the jagged edge and hauled himself upwards, inching his body over the ledge. He collapsed face first onto the icy surface, his chest heaving, gasping for breath. The cold bit into his skin, and the air – thinner, sharper, unforgiving – burned like fire in his lungs. It felt as though the mountain itself was punishing him for daring to climb this far.

For a brief moment, relief flooded his senses. He had made it.

He was alive.

The challenges of his journey seemed to slip away as he lay there, eyes closed, savouring the stillness. After rolling onto his stomach, he pushed himself slowly to his knees and lifted his head.

As he looked around, the sharp relief he had clung to just seconds before shattered into pieces, replaced by a wave of despair so heavy it nearly forced him back to the ground.

31

The Council

There was no summit.

No triumphant peak.

Just more cliffs, more jagged rocks, more endless mountain stretching ahead, vanishing into the mist like a cruel joke.

For a long moment, Andrew sat in stunned silence, grappling with the realisation. He thought of all the effort, all the courage it had taken to reach this point. His shoulders sagged and a tremor passed through him. He had given everything – *everything* – and yet it still wasn't enough.

He buried his face in his hands, the overwhelming fatigue and disappointment threatening to break him. But as he sat there, the faint sound of footsteps reached his ears.

Looking up, he gasped as he saw three familiar figures standing before him.

There, silhouetted against the mountain, were Santi, Sophia and Shuka, their expressions calm, filled with understanding. He blinked. Was he dreaming? But they were there, solid and real, watching him with quiet expectation.

Santi, ever the embodiment of warmth and joy, grinned as though he knew something that Andrew didn't as yet. Sophia's wise eyes held a spark of impatience, as if she were urging

THE TREE AND THE MOUNTAIN

him to seize the moment of discovery waiting just beyond his reach. Shuka's eyes reflected a profound understanding, a depth of sensitivity that reminded Andrew of everything he had buried but could no longer ignore.

They sat down in front of him, their faces glowing softly.

Santi gestured for him to join them and Andrew sank onto the cool stone, completing a circle that felt sacred, ancient and binding. The silence between them pulsed with unspoken truths, with the enormity of what had been left unsaid for far too long. Their presence wasn't demanding, but Andrew felt it nonetheless, like the sensation of being on the precipice of something inevitable.

When he finally spoke, his voice was barely a whisper. 'I've failed.' He looked at the ground. Saying it aloud made the truth heavier. 'I'm nowhere near the summit. I'll never see my kids or my wife again.'

The confession cracked something open inside him, and everything came rushing in… a flood of fear, regret and shame. His mind teemed with images… the missed birthdays… the hurried goodbyes at the door… the distant, half-listening moments at the dinner table. His daughter's voice echoed in his head: 'You're always busy, Dad.' And Lena, the love of his life, standing in the doorway with that familiar, resigned smile.

Santi's voice, gentle but firm, broke the silence like a lifeline thrown into turbulent waters. 'There's no failing, Andrew. Only falling down and getting back up again.'

Andrew's thoughts swirled like autumn leaves on the wind. 'How did you get here?' The confusion was raw in his voice.

THE TREE AND THE MOUNTAIN

'There are different paths up this mountain,' Santi answered simply.

Santi's words sank deep into Andrew's mind, like seeds waiting to grow. *Different paths.* How often had he assumed there was only one way forwards? He looked up at the towering mountain, its peak hidden beyond the clouds, extending beyond the limits of what he could imagine.

The realisation crept through him like a slow, dawning light... he had never actually seen the summit. He had been chasing the *idea* of it, driven by an image that existed only in his mind.

'What is this place?' he whispered, confused, his voice weary, carrying the burden of someone who had spent years seeking something he didn't fully understand.

Santi smiled gently, his hands pressing softly against the ground beneath him as if feeling the heartbeat of the mountain itself. 'This mountain has been here as long as you have.' His voice was full of reverence. 'It is the mountain of your youth, where your identity first took root. It's the place where you once explored life, through curiosity and wonder – before the world told you who you were supposed to be.'

Andrew held a breath. He could almost see himself as a child, climbing trees, running through open fields, driven by nothing but the pure joy of discovery. Before expectations crept in. Before success became a measure of worth and failure a looming shadow.

'It's where you learned to ask questions about who you are,' Santi continued, 'but over time, you stopped listening. The world convinced you to look outwards for answers.

Towards achievements... validation... status... And, slowly, you forgot this place.'

Andrew closed his eyes, the truth of Santi's words washing over him. He had spent so long climbing *up* that he had forgotten about the foundation he was climbing *from*. The boy who had once marvelled at the world had been buried under the man who needed to prove himself to it.

An ache of regret settled in his chest. 'I lost sight of the mountain.' His voice was barely a whisper.

'Yes,' Santi replied gently. 'But it never left you. It was waiting for you to remember it. When you heard that voice urging you to look beyond your tree, that was the moment you found it again – almost as if for the first time.'

Sophia's voice cut through the stillness. 'The mountain isn't a place or a goal to conquer. It's a path to remembering who you are.'

Shuka added softly, 'And the higher you go, the more you remember.'

Andrew's chest rose and fell, their words shifting something deep inside him. Yet, there was a barrier – a final truth hovering just out of reach. 'Is this real? Or am I dreaming it all?'

Santi smiled knowingly. 'What do you feel?'

Andrew closed his eyes, reliving the fear of the wolf pack, the storm that had nearly broken him and the warmth of the fire in the cave. He thought of Santi's wisdom, Sophia's guidance and Shuka's quiet strength. Every lesson, every emotion, every tear had felt unmistakably real.

'It's real,' he said firmly, opening his eyes. 'I feel it.'

Santi smiled. 'That's because you've stopped relying solely on your mind to define reality. You've learned to trust your heart. And that's the most real thing there is.'

Andrew's breath hitched. He had spent so long looking outwards for answers. Now the truth was here, sitting across from him, waiting to be acknowledged.

'Who are you?' he asked them, his voice barely above a whisper. 'And why are you helping me?'

Santi straightened, his gaze shifting to Sophia and Shuka before settling back on Andrew. His voice carried the gravity of something sacred.

'It's time you knew.'

32

Revelations

Santi took a breath. 'I'll begin. We first met beneath the oak, remember? You called on me when you needed to find connection and clarity. You were lost because you had overlooked me for too long. But I hold the keys to your energy, your alignment and your wisdom. I am... your heart.'

The revelation hit Andrew like a wave crashing over him, pulling him under. Moments they had shared flashed before his eyes: Santi's radiant smile... his profound insight... the unwavering guidance he had offered when he had felt lost. How could he have ignored this vital part of himself for so long?

Painful memories surfaced: the distant looks from his kids, Lena's unspoken disappointment and the friends who had drifted away. What mattered most had been pushed aside, neglected.

Santi had shown him how to reconnect with his core – his values, his talents and his aspirations. His Power of Nine. Andrew suddenly remembered Santi's parting words on the high ridge: *Listen to your heart. It is both wise and kind, and deserving of your trust.*

Tears welled in his eyes. He had asked Santi to guide him, but the truth was that Santi had always been with him, waiting for him to open the door – to embrace a heart-driven approach.

'It was me who abandoned you.' Andrew's voice was close to breaking. 'I'm so sorry.'

'There's nothing to forgive,' Santi said gently. 'You've found me now. That's all that matters.' The silence that followed was warm, healing.

Sophia spoke, her tone calm and compassionate. 'We met by the lake, remember? I am the second part of you that you called upon. I hold the keys to your operating system – your ability to navigate life, solve problems and execute plans. You relied on me for years, but you abused and misunderstood me.'

Andrew's breath caught in his throat.

'I am your mind,' she said softly.

Of course, he thought. She had helped him build the life he had pursued so relentlessly, blindly. *Always striving. Wanting more. Needing to prove himself. It never being enough.* But her exhaustion mirrored his own – years of overreaching without balance. She had been crying out for help, too.

Sophia, precise and unyielding, had guided him to a new understanding: that his over-reliance on the mind had hollowed him out; that decision-making was key to creating one's destiny; that sensitivity, far from a weakness, was a hidden superpower; and that the dialogue between the conscious and subconscious defined the narratives we cling to, shaping who we become.

REVELATIONS

Sophia's eyes shone with a quiet hope. 'You've pushed me too hard. I'm not meant to carry everything alone. My purpose isn't just productivity, it's to serve your heart. When it gives me direction, I thrive. But when you ignore your heart, I'm left running in circles, drained.'

Andrew nodded, a new sense of gratitude blooming within him. He remembered her parting words: *Let your heart guide, your mind execute and your energy speak. Together, they'll take you further than you've ever imagined.*

'I can see you now,' he said gently. 'And I will protect you.'

Sophia's smile softened, her relief evident.

Shuka's voice broke through, delicate yet strong. 'We met during the storm, when you felt completely lost. I guided you to the cave because you needed to reconnect with something you've hidden for years. I hold the key to your understanding of your fears, your self-belief and your inner confidence. I am the part of you that dreams, that hopes, that feels deeply. The part that never grows up... I am your inner child.'

Andrew's tears returned, falling freely. Shuka had carried the burden of his deepest fears: the fear of abandonment, of failure, of being unseen, unloved...

These drivers had led Andrew to forsake his heart and torment his mind, endlessly seeking the superficial comfort of external validation. Yet it had never been enough, had never been able to fill the void within. He had always felt inadequate whatever success he achieved. He had been searching in the wrong place all along.

Shuka had led him to the mountain, into the shadows. There, he had unveiled the gateway to a different kind of strength: the power to nurture a true and compassionate relationship with himself – one of love, recognition, belonging – cultivated from within, not stemming from the outside world.

Please don't forget me.

'I whispered to you as you clung to the tree,' Shuka said, with a gentle smile. 'I called you to this mountain because you were ready to remember.'

'I heard you. From now on, I will always hear you.'

Tears streamed down Andrew's face. He raised his sleeve to wipe them away, but Santi gently stopped him.

'I implore you not to wipe them away,' Santi said softly. 'Let them fall. These tears are the purest expression of your connection with who you are.'

Andrew let the tears flow, feeling lighter with each drop. He gazed at Santi, Sophia and Shuka, his heart, his mind and his inner child. They weren't just guides on his journey – they were parts of him, unified at last.

'I understand now,' Andrew said, firmly but gently. 'The summit I've been chasing isn't out there. It's here, within me. And I will carry it with me wherever I go.'

REVELATIONS

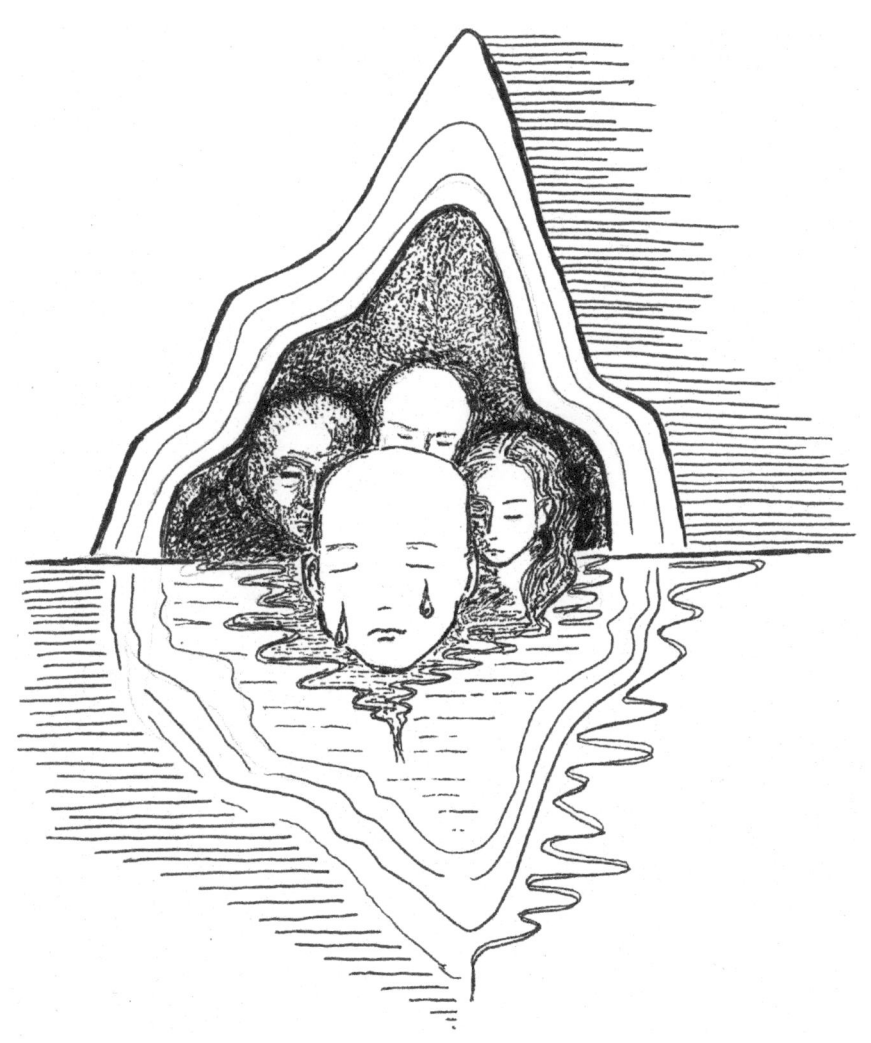

33

The Choice

Andrew's thoughts turned to the future – maybe, for the first time, without the insatiable desire to go higher and faster but rather deeper and more profound.

Lena, Oliver and Audrey's smiling faces emerged, as did his career and the offer of senior partnership.

What different choices would he make if given a second chance? And how would he get home?

Santi interrupted his musings. 'Andrew, the tree and the valley floor that you left behind… Do you understand what they represent now?'

Andrew nodded slowly. 'The tree is my career. The valley floor, the outside-only view I was entrapped by.'

'Indeed,' Santi said. 'The valley floor from whence you came is part of your past. You can never return there.'

The words sent a tremor through Andrew's spine. What did that mean? What would he have to give up? What about his tree, his career? Would he lose all that was familiar? A surge of uncertainty welled up in him, but before it could spiral, Santi raised a hand, signalling him to pause, to breathe.

'Your tree still exists,' Santi said, his tone grounding. 'But it is no longer where you left it.'

Andrew's thoughts became tangled. 'What do you mean? The tree is still back there, isn't it?'

Santi's gaze softened, a glimmer of encouragement in his eyes. 'No, Andrew. It's here. It has climbed with you.'

Andrew's confusion deepened, but then, almost instinctively, he looked beyond the three of them – and stopped cold. There it was. His tree. It was standing tall, rooted firmly in the mountain soil, its branches reaching for the sky, weathered yet vibrant.

'Of course…' His whisper was tinged with awe. The realisation struck him like sunlight breaking through a storm. 'The climb isn't about leaving everything behind. It's about integrating who I truly am into everything I do. *Inside out.*'

Santi's smile widened, the approval in his expression unmistakable.

Sophia's voice carried the next truth. 'Your tree will continue to grow, but it won't be the same as before. The soil here is different. The light is different. And you are different.'

Andrew felt a profound shift within him. His tree, rooted deeply in the mountain yet reaching upwards, was a perfect metaphor for everything he was beginning to understand.

The mountain was his truest self, the parts of him that ran deeper than any external label or accomplishment. The climb was his journey inwards. The tree and the mountain… an opportunity to connect the inner and the outer.

'Two sides of the same coin,' he whispered.

'Exactly so,' said Santi. 'It's like night and day, yin and yang, heart and mind. Nature thrives through harmony, and so do we. When your inner growth fuels your outer work

THE CHOICE

and your outer contributions reinforce your inner purpose, you create something extraordinary. They no longer exist in opposition… they flow together.'

A vision began to take shape in Andrew's mind. He saw himself at work – not driven by fear of failure or the need to prove himself but grounded in a sense of purpose. He imagined his relationships with Lena and the kids, no longer overshadowed by stress and distraction but filled with warmth, presence and authenticity. He saw his life not as fragmented parts but as a seamless whole, connected by a thread of meaning that ran through everything. *The purpose of being me*, as Sophia had reminded him.

Finally, Andrew turned to Santi, Sophia and Shuka, gratitude shining in his eyes. 'Thank you… thank you for showing me what I couldn't see on my own.'

They remained in silence for a time, the gravity of the moment filling the air until Sophia's calm voice broke through. 'You now have a decision to make, Andrew.' Her tone carried a gentle but undeniable finality. 'You can climb back up your tree. Or you can plant something new.'

Andrew's breath caught as he stared at the acorn in her open hand, small yet brimming with potential. He could sense its quiet hum of life, a promise of what it could become. He could almost feel it growing, its roots stretching deep into the mountain's soil, its branches unfurling towards the sky.

'What will you choose?' Shuka asked softly.

Just as he had done when clinging to the tree at the start of his journey, he took a deep breath.

THE CHOICE

His hands rose instinctively to rest over his heart – and he paused.

Grounding himself in the regular rhythm of his breathing, he turned to look up at the tree that had carried him this far – and paused again.

His heart pounded, just as it had when he had clung to the tree and looked out at the splendour of the mountain. Then he looked at the acorn resting in Sophia's hand, a seed of infinite possibility.

Finally, he closed his eyes, letting the noise of doubt and expectation fade. In the quiet stillness, three questions emerged within him like whispers carried on the wind:

What will help me live my values fully?

What will help me express my talents?

What will help me advance towards achieving my aspirations?

He let the questions guide him, his heart leading the way. As clarity bloomed from within, the truth revealed itself... simple and undeniable.

I know! I know!

He opened his eyes, his breathing steady, his hands resting on his heart.

Santi, Sophia and Shuka were nowhere to be seen. He looked down at his hands, only to find Santi's bracelet on his wrist. Andrew smiled. He knew exactly where they were.

He closed his eyes again and took a deep breath.

It was time to go home.

34

The Awakening

Beep. *Beep. Beep.*

The beeping grew louder, more distinct, pulling Andrew towards the surface of consciousness. It was rhythmic, constant, a lifeline cutting through the void, like the faint glow of a lighthouse guiding a lost ship. He drifted, his mind clawing for clarity, his body buried beneath what felt like endless layers of concrete.

I'm awake!

A flicker of determination ignited within him. He focused all his will on his toes, willing them to respond. At first, there was nothing but a crushing stillness. Then a twitch, subtle, faint but real. Relief flooded him like a cool wave. He wasn't gone. He wasn't entirely lost.

He latched onto that spark, shifting his focus to his hands, coaxing his thumb to flex. A small movement, barely perceptible but enough to confirm he was still here, still fighting. The effort exhausted him, but it brought hope.

He tried to open his eyes. They were heavy, like iron shutters rusted shut. He pushed harder, forcing them to part just slightly, only to be assaulted by blinding light. The fluorescent glare stabbed at his senses and he squeezed his eyes shut again, panting softly. Slowly, carefully, he tried once more, allowing the light to seep in as his vision adjusted.

Shapes began to form in the sterile glow: a stark white ceiling, a flickering neon light overhead, the cold gleam of metal rails on either side of him. The beeping was louder now, coming from machines that hummed and clicked, their tubes running into his arms. The air smelled sharp and antiseptic, sterile and unfeeling.

But then, as he shifted his gaze to the right, everything changed.

There, slumped in a plastic hospital chair, was Lena. His wife. Her head was resting against the wall, her face etched with exhaustion, even in sleep. Draped across her lap was Oliver, their son, all gangly and sleeping soundly, curled into his mother's legs. And leaning against Lena's shoulder was Audrey, their daughter, her thumb tucked into her palm, her cheek pressed to her arm. The three of them were a beautiful tangle of limbs, their peaceful stillness a stark contrast to the chaos that had raged within him.

Tears welled in Andrew's eyes, slipping down his cheeks as he took them in. He couldn't move. He couldn't speak. But he could feel – oh, how he could feel!

Overwhelmed by love, by gratitude, by the simple miracle of their presence, he let the tears flow freely. His family were here. They had stayed. They had fought for him.

As if sensing his awakening, Lena stirred. Her head tilted, her eyelids fluttering open. For a moment, she stared blankly, the fog of sleep clinging to her.

Then her gaze locked with his. Her breath hitched, her eyes widening as they filled with tears.

THE AWAKENING

'Andrew?' she whispered, her voice trembling. She shot upright, jostling both children awake in her rush to reach him. 'Oh my God, Andrew!'

Oliver and Audrey blinked, their sleep-clouded confusion melting into stunned joy. 'Daddy?' Audrey whispered, her voice tentative, disbelieving. When she saw his eyes open, her doubt shattered. 'Daddy!' she cried, leaping onto the bed, with Oliver close behind.

'Daddy! Daddy!' Their voices overlapped as they scrambled to hold him, their small arms wrapping around his shoulders, his chest, wherever they could find space. Their tears soaked his hospital gown, their small bodies pressing into him with an urgency that screamed, *Don't ever leave us again!*

Lena leaned over him, her hands cupping his face, her lips pressing soft, frantic kisses on his forehead. 'You're here,' she murmured between sobs. 'You're really here.' Her tears mingled with his as she held him close, as though her touch alone could tether him to life.

He tried to speak, his throat dry and tight, his voice buried beneath the effort it took just to breathe. But he forced his lips to move, rasping out a whisper. 'I'm here,' he managed, his voice weak but clear.

A nurse burst into the room, her eyes widening at the sight of him awake and surrounded by his family. Spinning on her heel, she called down the hallway: 'Doctor! Doctor! He's awake!' Her voice echoed down the sterile corridor, but Andrew hardly noticed. His world had shrunk to this room, to these faces, to these arms holding him so tightly.

THE AWAKENING

Oliver's voice cracked with emotion as he clung to his father. 'I missed you, Daddy. So much.'

Audrey's small hands clutched his chest as she cried into his gown. 'You're not going away again, right? You're staying with us?'

Andrew's heart broke and healed in the same instant. He wanted to pull them closer, but his body wouldn't obey. Instead, he met Lena's gaze. Her eyes were pools of relief, gratitude and an emotion so deep it defied words.

'I love you,' he whispered, his voice barely audible but loaded with everything he wanted to say.

Lena pressed her forehead to his, her tears falling freely. 'I love you too,' she whispered back, her voice thick with emotion.

The doctor arrived, followed by a flurry of nurses, their voices blending into the background. Andrew barely noticed as they checked his vitals, murmuring words like *remarkable* and *miracle*. His focus remained on his family, on the warmth of their touch, on the love that filled the room.

For the first time in what felt like an eternity, he felt at peace. The mountain, the storm, the wolves, the climb – all of it had led him back to this moment. To them. And to himself. To what truly mattered.

As the beeping of the monitors faded into the background, Andrew's chest rose and fell in a steady rhythm. He closed his eyes, not from exhaustion but from contentment, letting himself rest in the warmth of pure love.

'Everything is going to be OK,' he whispered.

Author's Note

The *Tree and the Mountain* is a story of deep introspection and hope, echoing the experiences of many who, unknowingly, have lost their way within themselves but harbour the belief that rediscovery is possible.

Through this allegorical journey, I aimed to impart profound messages via metaphor, convey essential learnings through character interactions and illustrate practical application through adventures and challenges.

The tree symbolises the career one builds over time, with the valley floor representing the 'outside-only' perspective that nurtured it. The mountain becomes the symbol of the 'real' self, while climbing it serves as a wondrous yet challenging journey to unveil one's true identity and improve how we choose to experience our life.

Three characters embody arguably the most powerful forces within us: the heart, the mind and the inner child. These characters developed unique features, traits and mannerisms emerging from my interactions with them. Even their names have significance:

Santi (Shanti) in Sanskrit means *peace, inner calm* or *tranquility*.

Sophia, in Greek, means *wisdom*.

THE TREE AND THE MOUNTAIN

Shuka (Śuka) is the child of a sage in Hinduism.

Today, I am frequently asked about the impact of my journey, with people essentially asking, 'What is it like to have one's tree on the mountain?'

In one word, it has been life-transforming.

These are the effects so far…

A perpetual state of tension and urgency has evolved into a state of flow and balance, where stress is the exception, not the rule.

My constantly active mind now remains focused, capable of switching on and off as needed and dedicated to the primary purpose of *being me* in my relationships, projects and work.

The fear of 'career collapse' – if I didn't perform – has shifted to an acceptance that each day is an invitation to be authentic and show up with energy to do one's best. Negative pressure has given way to positive pressure, which I embrace and enjoy.

Previously, I had no time for things I loved. Now, I *make* time. My relationship to time has transformed. We walk side by side rather than one behind the other.

Instead of being primarily future-focused, I concentrate on experiencing the present with awareness and awe. The future will wait for me. The present is where I choose to live my life.

No longer bent on proving something to someone, I view everything as an opportunity for self-discovery and discovery of others. Ironically, this approach leads to greater performance and impact through *flow* rather than *proving*.

AUTHOR'S NOTE

My energy, once depleting faster than it was being replenished, is now continuously regenerating from within, ensuring my best energy at work *and* at home for those I love the most: my wife and family.

The tired, frustrated shadow of my former self has been replaced by a dynamic, rejuvenated, authentic me, living in a healthy integrated system where everything of importance has its place.

It remains, by nature, a work in progress but such is the impact so far.

All this is achieved by learning to look deep inside, rediscovering the person that had been lost and forging a better path.

I wish you this and so much more.

Jonathan Cave

Chapter Learnings & Top Tips

Chapters 1–5: Discovering the Mountain

- Many of us are driven to ascend our career 'tree'.

- TOP TIP 1: Listening to and trusting yourself can unlock remarkable journeys of self-discovery.

- TOP TIP 2: When in doubt, breathing rhythmically gradually leads to stillness and a better sense of clarity.

Chapters 6–10: Meeting Santi

- Life's journey can serve to help us find or lose ourselves on the way.

- Answering the question *Who am I?* proves to be more challenging than it first appears.

- TOP TIP 1: Sharing your life story with another person is to give them a wonderful gift.

- TOP TIP 2: Listening to another human being intently and without judgement has a profound, connective effect.

- TOP TIP 3: Verbalising your deepest feelings can be a cathartic and healing experience.

Chapters 11 & 12: Nature's Energy

- The more we connect to nature, the more we discover our own 'nature'.

- Nature manifests three types of energy:

  (a) foundational energy, represented by roots in a tree or values in humans.

  (b) transformational energy, represented by photosynthesis in a tree or talents in humans.

  (c) directional energy, represented by multi-directional growth in a tree or aspirations in humans.

- Recognising these energies within ourselves helps us discover our 'central alignment line'.

- This virtual line – running through an imaginary axis at the core of our being – connects us to our high-energy, high-performing, authentic selves.

- TOP TIP: Consider making nature a prominent feature in your life, serving as a never-ending source of energy while helping you foster deep, regular introspection.

Chapters 13 & 14: Values

- Initiating a practice of closing one's eyes, placing our hands on our heart, and engaging in deep, rhythmic breathing opens the door to our inner selves.

- When we invite our heart to respond to important questions, and give it the space and time to do so, it imparts valuable wisdom.

CHAPTER LEARNINGS & TOP TIPS

- Our values are the non-negotiables that shape our behaviours, decisions and actions. They act as the foundational pillars of our house.

- TOP TIP 1: Identify your three core values to discover the foundational energy within that anchors you.

- A value is one energy. Applying it outwardly while neglecting to apply it inwardly splits this singular energy in two, generating a profound tension within us.

- TOP TIP 2: Actively apply your values to yourself to reduce stress while preserving core energy.

- When confronted with behaviours or situations that conflict with our values, we often tend to overreact, entering an uncontrolled, highly emotional state. There is nothing fundamentally wrong with us when we do. It is a natural reaction, which can, however, have negative consequences.

- TOP TIP 3: Consider learning to transition from a *reactive* mode (where emotions tend to be unidentified and uncontrolled) to a *responsive* mode (where emotions are identified and managed) to help calibrate your experiences while improving relationships with others.

Chapter 15: Talents

- Our talents are natural gifts we have received.

- They are usually effortless, come with a high personal enjoyment and often lead to important outputs.

- Many people don't know their talents because they are difficult to recognise in themselves.

- TOP TIP 1: Identify your three greatest talents to discover the transformational energy that helps you 'fly'.

- Arguably, the greatest talent anyone can have is to leverage their talents fully.

- Successful people tend to:

  (1) leverage their talents in everything they do and

  (2) surround themselves with people that have complementary talents.

- TOP TIP 2: Consider helping others find their talents, enabling them to tap into their transformational energy and propel their career and or business forward in a very natural, empowering way.

Chapter 16: Aspirations

- Aspirations are our desired future outcomes, representing the directional energy within.

- The multi-directionality of aspirations is represented by the trifecta of human existence: *being, doing* and *having*.

- TOP TIP 1: Identify your three deepest aspirations to tap into the directional energy that will propel you forward, by asking yourself the following questions:

  – Who do I want to BE more than anything?

  – What do I want to DO more than anything?

  – What do I want to HAVE more than anything?

CHAPTER LEARNINGS & TOP TIPS

- Those who are aware of their aspirations provide their lives with a clear direction, while those who lack this clarity are more susceptible to being carried aimlessly like a feather in the wind.

- TOP TIP 2: Consider transforming your aspirations into a yearly vision statement to keep them ever-present, helping you make choices that turn aspirations into reality.

Chapter 17: The Power of Nine

- The Power of Nine encapsulates the foundational, transformational and directional energy within us, represented by our three core values, three greatest talents and three deepest aspirations.

- Those values, talents and aspirations are component elements of our 'central alignment line', which gives access to our high-energy, high-performing, authentic self.

- TOP TIP 1: Visualise your Power of Nine every morning as you wake up to launch yourself into your day from a place of alignment, energy and clarity.

- *I am the master of my fate: I am the captain of my soul* said the poet, William Ernest Henley (1849–1903) in *Invictus*.

- TOP TIP 2: There are many paths to where we seek to go. Listening to your heart acts as a powerful guide. It is wise and kind. You can trust it.

Chapters 18 & 19: Meeting Sophia

- Nature operates in the present, being less concerned about future or past, rather about here and now.

- What life looks like on the outside is not necessarily how it feels on the inside.

- We can often hide our true feelings from others, preferring to keep them bottled up inside, afraid of what others might say or think.

- What most of us truly seek is simply a better path forward.

Chapter 20: The Mind

- The mind is a powerful supercomputer helping us determine what we need to do and in what order, from the moment we wake up to the moment we fall asleep every single day.

- The mind is primarily focused on performance, urging us to work harder, aim higher and accomplish 'more'.

- When left unchecked, the mind operates in a manner where we never seem to have time even when efficiencies are found.

- Our mind makes for a fantastic employee but a lousy boss.

- TOP TIP 1: Allow your heart to lead, your mind to execute and your energy to speak for you.

- Being heart-led directs the mind's insatiable desire for performance toward the noble purpose of being ourselves.

- TOP TIP 2: 'Be yourself; everyone else is already taken,' said Oscar Wilde.

Chapter 21: Decisions

- One way to align heart and mind is through the process of decision-making.

- We're often taught *what* to decide (what is practical and expected) not *how* to decide.

- The quality of our decisions significantly impacts the quality and trajectory of our lives.

- Exceptional decision-makers focus on clarity of *inputs* rather than certainty of *outputs*; on what they can influence instead of 'what if…' scenarios.

- TOP TIP 1: Developing a personalised decision-making process enables you to refine and optimise this critical skill, resulting in better personal and professional choices.

- TOP TIP 2: Some key questions to consider in building your decision-making process:

Information
  – What relevant information do I already have?
  – What critical information am I missing?
  – Where can I find that missing information?

External Perspectives
  – Which three people of trust can give me advice and/or honest feedback?
  – What other reliable resources can I consult?
  – How can they all help me avoid any blind spots?

Internal Perspectives
– What is my mind recommending?
– What is my gut warning me about?
– What is my heart whispering?

- TOP TIP 3: Power of Nine
Incorporating the nine reference points of your Power of Nine (three values, three talents, three aspirations) into your decision-making process ensures you continuously stay connected to your central alignment line.

  To do so, ask yourself the following: does each option help me…
  – align with my values?
  – express my talents?
  – progress towards my aspirations?

Chapter 22: Sensitivity

- High achievers often exhibit two key traits: *high intellectual capacity* (excelling in rapid information processing and systematic problem-solving) and *heightened sensitivity* (which involves perceiving the atmosphere, discerning energy without words and grasping sub-text through a finely-tuned radar).

- Many of us tend to suppress our sensitivity while overemphasising the intellectual, leading to an imbalance.

- Prolonged imbalance leads to losing our core identity, prompting a yearning for the suppressed sensitivity to emerge at some point in time (often mid-life or career).

- This emergence often takes two forms: a strong desire for creativity and/or a shift toward a heart-driven or more purpose-led approach.

- The challenge lies in restoring balance to our natural *high intellectual – heightened sensitivity* state.

- To achieve this, we are invited to learn tools to uncover and express our sensitivity, unlocking our deep intuitive state.

- When we do, our power of insight leads to foresight leads to wisdom.

- TOP TIP: Consider using tools such as visualising your Power of Nine or other self-discovery/introspective techniques to nurture sensitivity through alignment and energy.

Chapter 23: Internal Narratives

- The person we converse with the most in our lives is ourselves, hence the importance of internal narrative.

- Negative self-talk can erode confidence and deplete energy.

- Our internal narrative is significantly impacted by our conscious and subconscious minds.

- Our conscious mind governs voluntary actions and thoughts.

- Our subconscious mind governs involuntary actions and thoughts.

- Influencing the interaction between the two serves to transform internal narratives from negative to positive over time.

- TOP TIP 1: Incorporating affirmations like 'I believe in myself 100% today' into your daily routine fosters inner confidence and positive thoughts.

- TOP TIP 2: When negative thoughts surface, aim to disrupt them by consciously disagreeing with them as soon as they arise, to prevent infiltration into our subconscious.

Chapter 24: Meeting Shuka

- The condemning voices within us emerge particularly during times of stress, fear or vulnerability, often hindering our ability to act.

- Help often arrives when it's needed the most.

Chapter 25: Self-Belief

- Many people carry hidden fears, unknown to them and invisible to others.

- When explored, these fears reveal truths about our existence, including what is driving us forwards and holding us back.

- Exploring and understanding our fears allows us to address fundamental questions about our existence.

- Fear can serve as a powerful compass, but it often points us in the wrong direction.

CHAPTER LEARNINGS & TOP TIPS

- TOP TIP 1: Learning to transition from being 'fear-driven' to 'opportunity-driven' or 'potential-driven' is one of their most important journeys a person can make during the lifetime.

- TOP TIP 2: One practical way to do that is to learn how to discover, embrace and express our true selves in daily life, fulfilling our primary purpose of *being me*.

- Individuals with strong self-belief confidently recognise their self-worth, speak up more, ask for what they want and dare to be their true selves without fear of judgement.

- Individuals lacking self-belief often downplay their abilities, struggle to accept compliments, seek external validation and adopt roles to please those around them.

Chapter 26: Inner Confidence

- Many people appear confident on the outside but lack confidence and self-belief on the inside.

- We pursue fulfilment and achievement on the outside while neglecting to cultivate it on the inside, usually because no one taught us how.

- TOP TIP 1: Rather than relying solely on external achievements or others' perceptions (outside-in approach) for our value, contemplate a direct approach by fostering a stronger relationship with yourself (inside out).

- TOP TIP 2: Learn to give yourself what you've been searching for from others. Start from the inside and let it flow outwards. This will increase the likelihood of receiving that which you previously sought externally but did not receive enough of.

- By reclaiming ownership of our self-worth, which we may have delegated or abdicated to others, we bolster self-belief and learn to become our own reference point.

- It takes courage to be *you*. It also takes courage to be happy.

Chapter 27: Deep Fear

- Our deepest fears can surface at any time and in any place. We can choose to let them torment us or face them head-on.

- Going deep inside ourselves helps us access a power and a potential we have felt our whole lives.

- The more we accept who we are (including our history, our dreams, our desires), the more resilience we show.

- We can choose to face danger as the version of ourselves we would be proud of regardless of outcome.

- The phonetic form of *alone* is *al-one*, equating to being *all one* – connected to and within everything in the universe.

- TOP TIP: Consider learning to be *alone* to become *all one*.

Chapters 28–30: The Final Climb

- We will fall during our lifetimes. What makes the difference is our ability to get up and try again.

- A clear and powerful *why* underpins anything we do. It serves to energise and empower us, unleashing our full potential.

- The power of love can help us transcend insurmountable obstacles.

Chapter 31: The Council

- There is nothing more real than what we feel and think, nothing more authentic than who we truly are and what we experience.

- How we deal with deep disappointment reveals much about the strength of our character.

Chapter 32: Revelations

- The heart holds the keys to our identity and acts as the pathway to our energy, alignment and wisdom deep within.

- The mind holds the keys to our 'operating system' helping us navigate our daily existence and perform at our best.

- The inner child within holds the keys to our relationship with ourselves, as well as our inner confidence and self-belief.

- The act of crying helps us connect with ourselves, our tears being the only tangible proof of pure emotion that physically comes to the surface.

- TOP TIP: Consider appreciating tears for what they are: the very essence of who *you* are – and, as such, don't wipe them away.

Chapter 33: The Choice

- From a young age, we are conditioned to look *outside ourselves* for answers.

- This outward focus often drives us to pursue achievements, promising fulfilment and happiness. And while success can bring satisfaction, its impact is limited.

- TOP TIP 1: To overcome those limits, you are invited to look inward. By building a healthy, empowering relationship with yourself, you unlock a deeper source of strength and access lasting fulfilment.

- Our inner and outer worlds are interconnected. When they align, they form one integrated system, where purpose flows into action, and action reinforces meaning. This fosters a state of natural flow.

- TOP TIP 2: Look within. Make your choice.

Acknowledgements

To my wife, my soulmate... thank you for always believing in me, and giving me the time and space to write this book.

To my children... thank you for giving me the greatest gift I have ever received: the privilege of being your dad every day.

To my mum, dad and brother... thank you for your unconditional love and for standing by me in good and not so good times.

To my partner-in-crime, Cass Burgess, for your unwavering dedication as we build something meaningful together.

To my coaches and mentors, Martin de Waziers, Ravi Chaudhry, Sylvie Heritier, Feisal Alibhai and Nicolas von Burg... your care, your wisdom and your beautifully challenging questions have guided me more than you know.

To Olivia Dhordain... thank you for putting your unbridled, raw talent towards illustrating this book. I will be eternally grateful.

To my dear friends who read draft upon draft, thanks for your feedback and care.

To Cornerstones Literary Consultancy (Helen Corner-Bryant and Monica Chakraverty) and Myrmidon (Ed Handyside)...

thank you for believing in this book and helping bring it into the world.

Finally, to every reader holding these pages... this book is for you. May it accompany you on your own beautiful journey of becoming.

Ready for the next step?
Scan this code to explore Jonathan's
leadership and personal development
programmes and upcoming events.